SUPERVISORY SKILLS

for editors, news directors, and producers

SUPERVISORY SKILLS

for editors, news directors, and producers

Kevin M. Kelleghan

Iowa State University Press / Ames, Iowa

KEVIN M. KELLEGHAN is a bilingual trainer, author, and consultant. His career includes experience as a journalist for newspapers, magazines, wire services and radio and TV news, book publisher, foreign correspondent, newspaper and magazine editor, translator, columnist, television network executive, and manufacturer. He is fluent in Spanish. He's written three books and over 3,000 articles. He is a member of The Authors Guild Inc. and the American Society for Training and Development. He received a BA from St. Ambrose University.

© 2001 Kevin M. Kelleghan
All rights reserved

Important Caution to Reader: This book does not take the place of an attorney's advice.

Iowa State University Press
2121 South State Avenue, Ames, Iowa 50014

Orders: 1-800-862-6657   Fax: 1-515-292-3348
Office: 1-515-292-0140   Web site: www.isupress.com

Authorization to photocopy items for internal or personal use, or the internal or personal use of specific clients, is granted by Iowa State University Press, provided that the base fee of $.10 per copy is paid directly to the Copyright Clearance Center, 222 Rosewood Drive, Danvers, MA 01923. For those organizations that have been granted a photocopy license by CCC, a separate system of payments has been arranged. The fee code for users of the Transactional Reporting Service is 0-8138-0684-4/2001 $.10.

♾ Printed on acid-free paper in the United States of America

First edition, 2001

International Standard Book Number: 0-8138-0684-4

Library of Congress Cataloging-in-Publication Data

Kelleghan, Kevin M.
  Supervisory skills for editors, news directors, and producers / Kevin M. Kelleghan.—1st ed.
    p. cm.
  Includes index.
  ISBN 0-8138-0684-4 (alk. paper)
    1. Journalism—Management. I. Title: Supervisory skills. II Title.

PN4784.M34 K45 2001
070.4'068—dc21   00-056744

The last digit is the print number: 9 8 7 6 5 4 3 2 1

This book is based on information from sources believed to be reliable, and every effort has been made to make the book as complete and accurate as possible based on information available as of the printing date, but its accuracy and completeness cannot be guaranteed. Despite the best efforts of the author and publisher, the reader should use the book only as a general guide and not as the ultimate source of information about the subject of the book. This book is sold with the understanding that the publisher is not engaged in rendering legal or other professional services.

The book is not intended to reprint all the information available to the author or publisher on the subject, but rather to simplify, complement, and supplement other available sources. The reader is encouraged to read all available material and to learn as much as possible about the subject.

This book is sold without warranties of any kind, express or implied, and the publisher and author disclaim any liability, loss, or damage caused by the contents of this book.

Contents

Introduction   vii
Conventions Used in This Book   viii
Acknowledgments   ix

Section One: Managing   1

1 Improving Verbal Communication   3
2 Planning and Setting Goals   13
3 Distributing Work   25
4 Interviewing Job Applicants   35

Section Two: Motivating   55

5 Motivating Reporters and Managing Change   57
6 Making Presentations to Groups   75

Section Three: Mediating   89

7 Problem Solving and Decision Making   91
8 Handling Reporter Concerns   103
9 Dealing with Emotions   113
10 Counseling to Change Unsatisfactory Behavior   121

Section Four: Coaching   133

11 Conducting Performance Appraisal Interviews   135
12 Time Management for You and Your Staff   145
13 Coaching to Improve Competence and Performance   159
14 Team Building   167
15 Exceeding Customer Satisfaction   179
16 Training Reporters   185

Appendix   193
Index   197

Introduction

Although you've been promoted to your position, or hired, because of your journalistic ability, you'll be expected to manage your department from your first day with the competence of a seasoned, professional supervisor. Editors rarely receive training in supervision: Most textbooks for editors focus on writing and editing. As a member of the management team, however, you face a formidable challenge: The journalists you supervise are more independent than workers in other services or industries and often more difficult to lead with traditional management methods. The supervisory skills you practice must be adapted to the special needs of journalism.

How will you acquire those skills and still get the daily news report out on time? This book is your solution. It will prepare you for your new role, one for which you have the qualifications as a journalist but may lack the training as a manager. It will help you lead your newsroom to a new plateau of excellence in this era of constant change.

Some of the supervisory duties you will be expected to practice on a daily basis in addition to your editing responsibilities are

- Handling employee complaints
- Setting goals and objectives
- Interviewing and selecting candidates
- Assigning work
- Managing time
- Coaching and providing feedback
- Managing change
- Delegating
- Conducting performance appraisals
- Communicating and leading

You will be proficient in all of these management skills after studying *Supervisory Skills for Editors, News Directors, and Producers.*

Written by a 40-year veteran journalist, editor and publisher, this book is your introduction to the essential supervisory skills that every editor must master to achieve maximum effectiveness in the new media environment of the twenty-first century.[1] You will learn to manage people by understanding human nature. Each skill is presented in a succinct format: Here's why people act that way at work and here is what to do about it.

You get to-the-point instructions and solutions that succeed in any newsroom no matter what the medium: newspapers, magazines, radio, television, photography, electronic magazine, or news bureau.

The material in this book assumes you have little or no experience with management. While many editors will not need all the information in this book, an aspiring or newly-appointed editor certainly will. Although some of the information may be familiar to experienced editors, other sections may require repeated review. All the skills are essential for effective management of an editorial department.

The book is divided into four sections: Managing, Motivating, Mediating, and Coaching. They cover all the skills you will need to effectively supervise a newsroom staff.

While mastering the skills of effective leadership would be reward enough, the editor's role in today's media environment offers you more. An editor enjoys one of the most satisfying occupations in the field of journalism. Your position as an editor permits you to develop your talents and executive ability to their maximum creative potential to open doors to even more rewarding management opportunities.

Perhaps most exciting of all, because you work so closely with reporters, you are in an enviable position to exert a positive influence on the future of journalism.

A successful editor develops through four stages during the course of a fulfilling career:

1. Learning the skills of successful supervision
2. Practicing those skills at maximum potential
3. Improving those skills
4. Passing those skills on

Ultimately, your greatest satisfaction may result not so much from the knowledge, proficiency, and professional achievement that you acquire throughout your career as it will from what you share with those journalists you supervise.

Here, then, are the supervisory skills you need to help you do an important job well as an effective manager and an inspiring leader.

Conventions Used in This Book

The skills discussed in this book are useful for a person in a supervisory position at any medium: newspaper, magazine, radio station, television station, electronic magazine, and communications department in business, education, and government. They apply to supervision of people working in any capacity in the fields of journalism, information, and communication.

Because of the wide variety of job descriptions in these fields, the term *reporter* is used to refer to those who report to you. These include reporters, producers, photographers, broadcast news personnel, interns, and other persons you supervise. The term *reporter* is used most often to refer to all these job titles, although at times some or all job titles are listed.

All of the skills described here are essential, whether you work for a small company or a large organization, and whether you manage broadcast news or edit a print or electronic magazine. Forms are provided throughout the book for you to record your decisions and actions. Use of them is not a choice. You *must* keep detailed records of everything you say and do with those who report to you. This cannot be overemphasized. If human resources professionals agree on one thing, it is that in an increasingly litigious society, documentation is mandatory.[2]

The critical role of planning is emphasized throughout the book. In your capacity as a journalist, you worked on a story as it developed. For the most part, plans were superfluous because people and events beyond your control could change them. Pilots are taught to plan the flight, then fly the plan. As an editor, you are encouraged to do the same: Plan carefully, then stick to your plan. And always be prepared for the unexpected.

Acknowledgments

Several people took time from their busy schedules to review this book to assure its accuracy and timeliness. Any errors, however, are mine alone. I thank Steve Schinzer, veteran trainer and author of a management training course, for his invaluable assistance with abundant research materials and documentation from the moment this book was conceived until the final draft. I thank Fran Church, human resources consultant, for her incisive and thorough review and her insistence on the importance of documentation. I thank David G. Burch, human resources consultant, for his encouragement and suggestions for the tone of the book. I thank June Taylor, editor extraordinaire, for her eagle eye in catching and correcting lapses in the use of the language. I thank Charles H. Green, Director, International Journalism Center, Florida International University, for his insight and guidance as a journalist and as a supervisor. His assistance helped maintain the focus on journalism as well as supervision. And I thank the competent professionals at the Iowa State University Press for shepherding this book from the initial proposal to the final printed volume, and all the guidance and correction in between. Above all, I thank the ultimate source of the information in this book, divine inspiration, without which this book would not even exist.

Note

1. In the new media environment of the twenty-first century, reporters, producers, photographers, or broadcast news personnel assume a wider role in the administration of the newsroom, an environment in which technology will heavily influence as well as continually change the way you do business.

2. This book is not intended to nor provides legal advice or advice regarding legal ramifications of any matters discussed. Readers are encouraged to consult with legal counsel with respect to these issues. Moreover, it is impossible to foresee all possibilities of the application of the information in this book or the degree of understanding and proficiency of each reader. Consequently, the reader agrees to hold the author and ISUP harmless for any consequences, legal or otherwise, that result from any action taken from using information in this book.

SECTION ONE

Managing

1 Improving Verbal Communication

After you finish this chapter, you will be able to:
- Evaluate your communication skills
- Practice effective verbal communication
- Improve your listening skills
- Practice the Ten Commandments of Effective Communication

Introduction

Verbal communication in a newsroom is an intricate web of paths to and from each person who reports to you. So vital is verbal communication that one textbook on management affirms it is the adhesive that unites all other management functions. Research shows that 70 percent of all problems in a business can be traced to faulty communication. Yet the typical editor devotes less effort to developing and improving this skill than to any other.

One tenet of effective communication requires that all parties understand and agree on the meaning of terms. So, let's begin by defining the term *communication*. How would you define communication? Write at least four words or phrases that you would use to define *communication*.

1. _____
2. _____
3. _____
4. _____

You may have written words such as *inform, feedback, give-and-take, exchange information, discuss, talk,* or *report.* You may also have written down *listen.*

The origin of the word *communication* may help flesh out your definition. *Communication* comes from the Latin *communicare,* or connected, and *communis,* or common. *Comm* appears in many languages: Spanish, French, and Italian, as well as English. The word in Spanish for common is *común*. Let's add this key point to the definition we are developing: *Communication* means *connected: to share something in common.*

When a communication is successful, both sides are connected to the same message, understand it, and therefore *share* it. Understanding is validated when the receiver of a verbal message can repeat the message in his or her own words.

The basic theory of communication is deceptively simple, yet its successful practice is amazingly complex:

Sender ———————→ Message ———————→ Receiver

The speaker sends a message to a receiver. The receiver acknowledges the message with feedback:

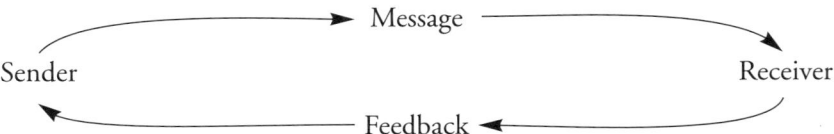

Although communication would appear to be easy to accomplish, the road that even the simplest message travels from one person to another is littered with obstacles. Too often the receiver modifies, interprets, or changes the meaning that the speaker, or sender, intended to convey.

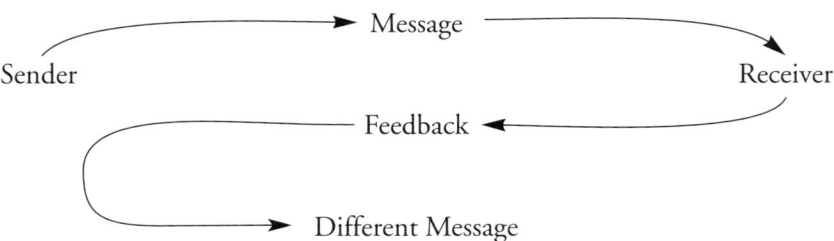

The Importance of Effective Communication

Effective verbal communication between you, as an editor, and each reporter, producer, photographer, or broadcast newsperson who reports to you is so important that it can easily contribute to the success of all your other supervisory activities. One study showed that an amazing 60 percent of all misunderstandings are due to poor listening. Another study revealed that 80 percent of all business communication must be repeated. As if that weren't enough, only 20 percent of what top management says is understood five levels below.

Good communication requires planning, concentration, constant attentiveness during a conversation, elimination of distractions, and clarification of terms throughout. Few people excel at clear, concise, and correct verbal self-expression. On the other hand, a person may understand a simple message yet be unable to repeat it back in a coherent sentence. This can be true even of reporters who are capable of communicating clearly in writing. Even those who sincerely believe they are good communicators frequently interpret or modify a message to conform to what they want to hear.

To complicate matters even more, a variety of other influences can alter the meaning of a message. For example, listeners seldom hear a message objectively. They unconsciously manipulate and interpret information. Their background, gender, education, quirks, sense of humor, values, place of origin, and other factors can all affect how they hear a message. Research shows that people hear what they want to hear. They filter, even obstruct, what they don't want to hear and then mold what they do hear to match what they already believe. Table 1.1 on page 6 lists just a few of the filters that a listener can use, quite unconsciously, to modify a message.

Eight Tips to Improve Your Communication Skills

An effective communicator makes sure each message is clear and understood. These suggestions can help you make sure the message you send is the message your listener receives and that you, in turn, understand the messages you receive.

Agree on the Meaning of the Words You Use

The same word can mean different things to different people. Make sure your listener knows how you are using words and agrees to the same meaning. For example, the word *torch* means flashlight in England. A *lift* is an elevator in England. Assigning the same meaning to words can be especially relevant when different generations communicate. To make certain both sides of the conversation have understood the same thing, summarize what you stated when you finish a conversation, then ask your listener to do the same.

Table 1.1 Filtering

Filters	Consequences
EXPERIENCE	Two people can discuss the same activity and yet reach different conclusions based on their past experience. *Example:* You say to a reporter, "I spent last evening reading." You are referring to work-related reading. The reporter may interpret your statement to mean you read a novel, since that is what the reporter does when the reporter "spends an evening reading." Based on the experience each of you has had in the past, you can interpret the same word differently. Unless one of you expands and clarifies the information—"I spent the evening reading work-related reports," for example—the other may not know how to interpret your statement and so will filter the statement based on personal experience.
EXPECTATIONS	Your reporters expect you to react a specific way because you have consistently reacted that way in the past. *Example:* If reporters are subjected to intolerance or sarcasm when they make mistakes, they will expect similar treatment again when they goof. They might dread reporting what could be a costly error because they expect the editor to demean them again. Reporters normally don't share their expectations with their bosses. What's more, chances are the editor will never learn about the reporter's expectations because people rarely reveal expectations until they are transgressed.
FEARS	No matter how they're described, all fears fall into one of two categories: 1. Fear you won't get something you want. 2. Fear you will lose something you have. *Example:* A reporter and you recently discussed a wage increase, but concluded nothing. Today, you call the reporter to your office to notify him about a change in printer usage due to a breakdown after especially heavy use recently, and to set new guidelines for using the printer. The reporter was the person who last used the printer and the topic is unrelated to the wage talks, but when you called him into your office, the reporter feared the printer damage would affect wage negotiations or even his job. As the reporter listened to you, he realized with relief that both fears were unfounded, and paid scant heed to your instructions. With great relief, he returned to his work station and wondered, "Now, what was the limit of sheets the editor said I could print at one time?"
SENSE OF HUMOR	One person may be jocular while the other person in the conversation is serious. The person with the sense of humor may seem to treat just about everything lightly, a trait that does not amuse the serious person. *Example:* You may have a keen sense of humor and like to tell jokes. In contrast, one of the reporters in your newsroom is quite serious. You begin a conversation by telling a joke, an ice breaker, to preface a serious

conversation. The serious reporter listens to your joke, but doesn't get the punch line and asks you to explain, which you do. By now, the serious reporter is wondering what that joke has to do with the topic under discussion. Communication, or connecting, never really gets started.

PREFERENCES   People have higher energy levels and work more efficiently at certain times of the day. They may be more receptive during those times as well. *Example:* Some reporters are morning people, while others are much more alert in the afternoon. You may get a person's fullest attention only after she has had that first cup of coffee in the morning.

Provide Continuous Feedback During Every Conversation

Acknowledge you are listening by using verbal clues such as "I see." You might nod your head or say "uh-huh" to signal that you are giving the speaker your full attention. Take advantage of pauses to summarize what was just said.

Plan Your Message Ahead of Time

Take a few moments to mentally review what you plan to say. Organize your thoughts beforehand so that you can introduce the topic and then discuss it.

EXAMPLE

You begin a conversation with, "Cut the number of long distance calls and spend less time when you call out of state." Reporters might misinterpret that order and not make important calls. If you had planned the conversation, you might have begun with, "Our long distance phone bill last month was much higher than budgeted. Therefore, I am going to ask each of you to make sure every long distance call is necessary, so we can bring the bill back in line with our budget." Try to summarize the thoughts that preceded your message so that the message itself is clear. An introduction helps listeners understand the thought process that led up to the message.

Limit Your Topic

If you try to accomplish too much in one conversation, your listener may select certain topics and remember only those. Therefore, it is best to discuss just one topic at a time. If you have two topics to discuss, conduct two separate conversations. If you must discuss two topics in the same conversation, finish one before beginning the second.

Set a Goal for Each Communication

Decide in advance what you want to accomplish. Then make sure your listener understands the purpose of your communication. You can't expect your listener to arrive with you at a specific destination if the listener doesn't know where you're going.

Anticipate Questions

This is one of the most effective, and least utilized, techniques for saving time while improving communication. Try to determine what questions your listener might have and prepare your answers in advance. How often have you heard a superior say, "I don't have the answer but I'll get back to you"? How many times did that superior actually get back to you? If you prepare for questions your listener might ask, you won't have to get back with the answer, which could delay or even undermine your objective.

Keep Distractions to a Minimum

When you're speaking in your office with a reporter about an important subject, set your phone to receive voice mail and ban drop-in visitors. This simple technique shows the reporter you consider the conversation important. Although you may not think so, all meetings with the boss are important to an employee. The reporter ought to feel that he or she is the most important person at that moment. This is an exceptionally powerful way to get a listener's attention because it flatters the listener's ego. Eliminating distractions also emphasizes the importance of the topic. Finally, it will ensure your own as well as the other person's concentration.

Recognize Authority Levels

Although you may strive for a certain level of camaraderie between you and those who report to you in the newsroom, and may in fact develop close friendships with some reporters, the fact that you are the boss is never far from any reporter's mind. Consequently, it is unwise to banter too much. People expect you to fulfill your role as supervisor. On a bad day, they may be unduly sensitive and may misinterpret your kidding and take offense. Others may take advantage of the close friendship with you to exact favors from colleagues, or take advantage of you in subtle ways. Strive to draw a line between friendship and job responsibility so that the difference is understood and respected by all who report to you. The ability to make this distinction clear is one of the hallmarks of a true leader.

Listening

Test your listening skills by completing Table 1.2 on page 10.

The Ten Commandments of Exceptional Listening

1. Be as open and forthright as you expect the reporter to be.
2. Mentally outline key points as you listen.
3. Reserve judgment until you have heard the reporter out.
4. Accept that the reporter may think a different viewpoint is correct.
5. Try to understand the reporter's point of view.
6. Wait until the reporter finishes to decide what your response will be.
7. Try to listen to the emotions *behind* the words.
8. Avoid mental wandering when listening: Stay focused.
9. Consider the reporter's viewpoint when replying.
10. Avoid interrupting when the reporter is speaking.

Five Causes of Inefficient Listening

People use only half their capacity when listening, according to research. Besides that, many factors hinder effective listening, among them selective memory, internal chatter, distractions, environment, and the speaker's tone of voice.

1. *Selective memory.* People choose the information they want to remember, usually information that agrees with their preconceptions. They can forget or even ignore information that doesn't.
2. *Internal chatter.* The thinking that goes on in our heads while others are speaking can be distracting. We speak at about 125 to 150 words a minute, but listen (or think) at about 600 to 750 words a minute. The difference creates a vacuum that is usually filled with extraneous thoughts that may be irrelevant to the present conversation. The chatter can override what is being said. A listener may be worrying about a toothache, watching the clock for the next appointment, or

Table 1.2 How Well Do You Listen to Those Who Report to You?

Check your answer on the right	Rarely	Sometimes	Usually
1. I reserve judgment about the speaker until I hear everything that the person is trying to say.			
2. I recognize I may hold a strong point of view and allow for it when I listen.			
3. I try hard to understand the reporter's point of view.			
4. I wait until the reporter finishes speaking before I reply.			
5. I try to listen to the "emotional content" as well as the words when speaking with those who report to me.			
6. I try not to let my mind wander to urgent matters when reporters are speaking with me.			
7. I give reporters positive feedback during conversations.			
8. I avoid interrupting when a reporter is speaking hesitantly, and I avoid attempting to anticipate the reporter's thoughts.			
9. I avoid using language calculated to impress.			
10. I speak loudly enough to be heard and do not put down my listener when I am not understood.			
Totals			

If you marked:

Usually 10 times: You are a considerate and effective communicator with reporters.

Sometimes 5 times or more: Your communication with reporters will improve if you allow them more time to express themselves.

Rarely 3 times or more: You could improve your communication skills by practicing The Ten Commandments of Exceptional Listening.

wondering what to prepare for dinner tonight, and miss hearing important information, then be at a loss when asked for a replay.
3. *Distractions.* Distractions affect our ability to pay attention to messages. External distractions such as a telephone ringing, a siren, or someone passing by behind the person speaking are obvious ones. Other, more subtle internal distractions include hunger (the listener may be more concerned with lunch than the message), anger (which can affect how the message is received), fatigue (one of the parties may be too tired to pay attention), and discomfort (a hard chair can do that). Any of these conditions make concentration difficult.
4. *Environment.* A room that is too hot or too cold can demand a person's full attention and get in the way of connecting and sharing a message fully.
5. *Tone of voice.* Tone, modulation, loudness, and emphasis can affect how a listener hears a message. The meaning of a serious statement may be altered, for example, by a humorous tone.

Five Tips for Better Listening

Communication problems might be eliminated if people would only pay full attention when they listen. Effective listening requires concentration not only on the words being used, but also on the meaning behind those words.

1. Keep clarifying as you listen until you understand the message.
2. Force yourself to concentrate on what's being said.
3. Mentally list key points and outline what's being said.
4. Don't concentrate only on what you want to say.
5. Interrupt only when you don't understand what is being said.

Eliminating Problems in Communication

Some editors will not tolerate disagreement. This often occurs when the editor fails to respect a different point of view. As editor (and boss), you can recognize and respect another person's point of view even though you do not agree with it. Two different points of view do not necessarily make one person "right" and the other "wrong." Both sides can sincerely believe they have the right position (and they usually do when they argue or they wouldn't defend it so vehemently). As a supervisor, try to understand that neither side is necessarily wrong. Both sides may well be right—they are just different. Try to understand the other person's point of view before rejecting it, if it opposes yours.

As an editor, you cannot afford to block information that your reporters try to convey to you. It is essential that you be open to whatever they want to say.

In the next chapter you will study the management skills that communication binds together. You will use them continuously to manage your newsroom and inspire your staff.

2 | Planning and Setting Goals

After you finish this chapter, you will be able to:
- Set attainable goals for your newsroom and your people
- Communicate your expectations and motivate reporters to strive to achieve them
- Help reporters set goals to improve their efficiency and productivity
- Monitor reporters' progress in achieving goals

Introduction

One generally accepted definition of a supervisor is someone who gets things done through others. To accomplish this the supervisor practices four basic management functions: planning, organizing, directing, and controlling.[1] From managing people to managing the news report, you will use all these skills as an editor to accomplish your objectives for your newsroom. In a large media company, senior management usually takes care of planning and organizing, while editors (in their role as supervisors) handle directing and controlling. But in a smaller organization, you may well find yourself carrying out all four functions.

Planning is by far the most important of the four management functions because how well everything else goes is a consequence of it. Planning begins with considering alternatives before deciding on a course of action. Although the best choice will often be apparent, you'll face hard decisions many times when no one option seems attractive. A useful Planning Formula that can help you evaluate courses of action is described below.

As you plan, whether for a project or a story, decide what you want to achieve—your objective—and write it down in language that is clear, concise, and specific. With a goal in place, your plan is more likely to move in the direction you envision. Next, communicate your plan and goal to everyone involved. Ideally, each participant will agree to both.

Organizing is the second management function. When you organize, start by selecting the elements that you feel will contribute to the result you want to achieve, choosing from among all the elements at your disposal in your department. This includes personnel, equipment, and anything else that will be needed. Before you finish your organization, look at the relationship of each item to every other item (how the individuals get along with each other as a team, for example). Finally, allocate tasks to carry out the desired goal, including the specific tasks that each individual or department will carry out to contribute to the goal. This organizational phase can be as detailed as you like, such as each individual's work space in the office.

Directing is the third management function. After you have selected the right people for the job, your role is to provide direction as the plan is carried out. Because directing always involves people, effective leadership is a vital element. Although you don't need to be born with this trait (many editors develop into superb leaders) you should know what effective leadership looks like. That's not simple because leadership is not easy to define. It's easier to describe what a leader does: An effective leader motivates, inspires, and persuades reporters to contribute willingly to goals at their maximum competence. As an effective leader you must also practice what you preach, treat everyone who reports to you equally, maintain high standards of personal ethics, discipline fairly, and recognize effort and application often and generously.

Controlling, the fourth management function, incorporates three elements: people, materials, and budget. You guide both people and results with a system of controls you devise to direct your plan to successful completion. These controls are standards for performance that everyone will adhere to willingly as the plan is carried out. The standards become your tools for measuring performance so that you can correct any deviations from them. Controls also provide early warnings of problems that could prevent the plan from producing its expected result. Your budget is a good example of a tool to control spending.

We look at planning and goal setting in this chapter. The functions of organizing, directing, and controlling the efforts of reporters, producers, photographers or broadcast news personnel, as well as project management, are covered in the balance of this book.

Planning Formula

Here's a step-by-step formula you can use to plan a project. Although it was inspired by standard management practice, we have adapted it here to the special needs of journalism. What's most attractive about this planning formula is that its principles are already familiar to you. The formula incorporates four of the five "Ws" of writing a story and adds two more.

To determine a course of action, ask yourself the following questions:

1. What will be done?
2. Who will do it? Will this person be accountable for the project's success?
3. Where will it be done?
4. When (deadline) will it be done?
5. How will it be done?
6. What can go wrong?

Goal-Setting

Your plan is more likely to succeed if you set a goal for it. The chances for a quality story being done right the first time increase greatly if you communicate the why (the goal) as well as the what (the activity) of the task. On the other hand, if you fail to establish a clear objective, participants may not be certain of where they're going. They may feel that any road will take them there, but they may not know where they are when they get there.

Goals fit into two categories: general or specific. A *general* goal might be what you want to accomplish and where you want to take your people and your newsroom over a three-year period. A *specific* goal focuses on a particular project or a particular reporter, such as

- Number of stories produced each day
- Maximum time dedicated to learning new skills, for example, a new IT^2 application
- Time devoted to writing and turning in a story
- Quality of writing
- Personal time management during the day

Helping Reporters Set Goals

When I was manager of a newspaper, I found that goal-setting was a skill that every reporter needed to learn. It increased productivity tremendously, from one story to three per reporter per issue. But editors rarely teach reporters goal-setting skills. Many think that the story assignment is the only goal the reporter needs because they mistakenly assume all assignments will be handled efficiently.

Most reporters have an innate instinct for setting a goal for a story. But there are a few who don't have that capability. These people may often spend unproductive hours chasing blind leads or making pointless phone calls. To get such reporters to work on improving their effectiveness and to enhance their productivity, encourage them to set a clearly defined goal for each story.

Perhaps you have already attempted to teach reporters how to manage a story more efficiently and were disappointed by the results. You may be reluctant to try again. You might have been disappointed because the reporters didn't use methods that have worked for you. This can happen when editors insist on the same perfection from reporters that they demand from themselves. In such cases, editors need to understand that each reporter works differently. Reporters aren't doing their work wrong because their style is different from yours. Once you accept that there is no one "right way" to handle a story, you can adapt to the reporter's style and work with that. The secret of success is not to insist reporters work in a certain style, but rather to work with each reporter's unique style and help improve that. Rather than insist on perfection, encourage the reporter to *strive* for perfection.

On the other hand, the difficulty in getting reporters to discipline themselves by setting and adhering to goals may simply be a matter of poor communication. You may fail to share your expectations with your staff. You may fail to tie the goal to your expectations. Or you might never have set goals in the first place for yourself, for your newsroom, your news report, or those who report to you.

Besides setting the goal, you must make sure the reporter understands your expectations. These must be measurable expectations that the reporter can achieve.

Time constraints or heavy demands on your attention may discourage you from teaching goal-setting techniques to the reporters in your newsroom, or you may feel that the reporters should already know how to set goals. However, the time you spend teaching goal-setting skills will be well worth the investment for both you and the reporters.

Reporters who set goals

- Produce more stories each day
- Develop stories with more depth and quality
- Finish stories sooner
- Consistently turn in stories before, rather than at, deadline

Planning a Story: The ROAD Method

One effective system for managing the planning phase of a story is a method I adopted for a magazine when I was editor-in-chief, the ROAD method: resources, obstacles, action, direction.

- *Resources.* Three types of resources are involved in planning a story: information, means, and time. *Information* refers to the contact and background information—the database—available for the story. This would include the names, addresses, and phone numbers of sources, articles on the topic in the morgue, research such as Web searches, other people to interview for balance, photo opportunities, and any other available information. *Means* is threefold: the time, assets, and budget you are willing to commit to the story. *Time* is controlled by deadlines; *assets* include people and equipment such as PCs or laptops, telephones, and vehicles; and *budget* is the amount of money you can commit to covering the story. A major story may require a considerable investment, for example. Funds are not limitless so the cost of a story, especially a complex one, needs to be estimated.
- *Obstacles.* People or situations could interfere with or prevent the reporter from gathering the necessary information for the story. You'll save time and improve your chances of success if, during the planning stage, you consider what obstacles you may face and how to overcome them.
- *Action.* This is the cluster of decisions, and their sequence, that you need to make: assigning reporters to the story or shaping teams to handle different aspects; equipment to commit; deadlines; writers; editors; photographers; and any other decisions.
- *Direction.* You decide on the angle for the story and establish standards and controls.

Planning for Unforeseen Events

Always expect that something you never thought of will happen. That way you will more likely get through even the most difficult assignment. No matter how thoroughly you plan, assume that some things will go wrong. For example, when I worked at the Associated Press bureau in Mexico City, the bureau chief planned for the first visit of Pope John Paul XXIII to Mexico. Then the bureau chief planned again. He was prepared to be flexible, to deal with any contingency. Even with all that careful foresight, problems developed: Traffic jams slowed film delivery, weather delayed the landing or takeoff of the chartered jet. Yet Bureau Chief Chuck Green said he was able to cover that story without problems because he planned for the unexpected.

Coverage of the Winter Olympics in Lake Placid is another good illustration. Even with careful planning to cover every event and meet every contingency that the bureau could think of, no one ever dreamed the American team would beat the Russian ice hockey team. As a result, the

AP had to pull people in from other assignments to cover the story. Fortunately, Bureau Chief Chuck Green had learned from his Mexico experience and had insisted that the AP keep an extra person in the newsroom as a standby in the event of an emergency.

Expect to be surprised by events that never occurred to you when you made your plans. This is one area of management practice that seems to be unique to journalism, since the world of business insists that there should be no surprises.

Effective Goal-Setting

Whether you are planning a story for one reporter or the day for everyone in your newsroom, you need to know what makes a goal effective.

An effective goal is clear, realistic, flexible, and accepted. That is, everyone clearly understands and acknowledges the goal; everyone can achieve the goal; the goal can be adapted or modified to changes in conditions; and everyone involved agrees with, accepts, and commits to the goal willingly. Even if it is not enthusiastic, commitment is essential. You want reporters to accept the goal even when they disagree. Otherwise, you might face a situation in which some people reluctantly do what they're told because they are ordered to, but may later gripe and even sabotage a plan.

Clear Goals

You may sincerely believe that the instructions you give to a reporter are simple and straightforward, subject to only one interpretation. Yet the reporter may leave a conversation with you with a different perception. Through a process called *filtering,* people frequently alter the information they hear to make it conform to something they want to hear, or to match a preconceived idea. Reporters can misinterpret your goal by deciding to hear something in a different way than the way you present it. Let's look at an example.

In a meeting with a reporter, you describe the information you have for a story and your expectations for it. As the reporter listens to you, she mentally envisions a different focus. As you speak, the reporter filters what you say, deciding to pursue this different aspect. The reporter filters out your vision, replacing it with her personal one. Your point of view may be rejected, ignored, not heard, not even considered. The reporter hears what you are saying but is *filtering* it.

You won't know when a reporter is mentally filtering information, but you can do something to counteract it. After you finish discussing the assignment, ask how the reporter plans to pursue the story. Don't lead; let the reporter tell you what he or she plans to do *in the reporter's own words*. As you listen, be alert for even subtle differences that might hint at a different direction or might change what you said into something slightly off the mark.

Realistic Goals

Some goals may exceed a reporter's willingness to accept an assignment or ability to carry it out competently. In other cases, employees say the words they think the boss wants to hear, even when they disagree. Others don't know how to say no. A few may not speak up even when they feel the boss expects too much from them.

To avoid these possibilities, make sure your people

- Understand that you expect them to meet a goal
- Understand that you expect them to reveal any reservations they have

For example, if this is a person who might be reluctant, you could say, "I know you can do this assignment, but I want to be sure you're comfortable with it. Do you foresee anything that you think might prevent you from carrying this out?" If the reporter asks you to explain, you can be direct and specific: "Are you working on stories right now that I am not aware of?" or "Do you think this is not really your beat? Do you think someone else ought to do this?" Bear in mind that you're not giving the reporter a chance to reject the assignment by doing this (unless that is your objective); you're offering the reporter a chance to voice any reservations.

Flexible Goals

It certainly isn't news to you that stories don't always work out the way an editor initially envisioned them, for all sorts of reasons. Sometimes a reporter may not move on a story fast enough to suit an editor, or may fail to get enough information, or can't document it. Occasionally, plans are simply canceled by an editor's superiors with no explanation and little notice. So you always need to remain flexible and prepared to alter your objectives or deadlines, or assign different personnel.

Changes can create new problems among personnel if they are not explained when appropriate. Your staff needs to know when their work is unsatisfactory and needs improvement, and should be told, of course. But they also need to be reassured when the change has nothing to do with the quality of their efforts since some people tend to take things personally and blame themselves for such changes. You can avoid such assumptions by making clear, open, detailed, and frequent communication an essential element of your management style from your first day as editor.

Accepted Goals

Editors can be disappointed when goals are not met exactly as envisioned, a problem that frequently results from their failure to discuss expected results in specific terms when goals are first set. Reporters may not accept a goal or have reservations but remain silent. Or they may need more information or clarification. Gaining acceptance is important, not because you're pleading for agreement, but because silent indifference or vocal opposition can undermine your plans, and you may never know it. You're not trying to convince them; you're making sure they're committed.

To make sure your goal is accepted, involve the reporter in setting it. Chances for enthusiastic commitment increase because the reporter will take ownership of the goal if he or she contributes to creating it. If at all feasible and time permits, ask the reporter to contribute suggestions as you jointly establish the goal and the plan to meet it. This is a much more practical method than simply dictating plans yourself. You might even allow the reporter to present an alternative idea for the story.

There are several additional benefits to involving reporters in the process. First, you'll encourage creativity and commitment. Second, you'll be able to assess the process the reporter uses to cover a story, which can help you determine the reporter's potential for promotion.

Unless they have questions, in most circumstances reporters will simply respond "Yes, sir" or "Yes, ma'am," and get back to work after receiving instructions. Reporters may remain silent even when they feel they lack competence to carry out your instructions or feel you are demanding too much. The reporter's body language may not always reveal to you that the reporter doesn't like what he or she hears. You may not find out about a negative reaction until later, when productivity dips. Some reporters may grumble to colleagues, but you won't be aware of it. Journalists seem to have a penchant for complaining. Others are just chronic whiners. If you suspect a reporter is not in full agreement, take the time to discuss the reporter's uncertainty. Use your motivational skills to generate enthusiasm. Enthusiastic commitment is always better than resigned acceptance, even if it takes longer to attain.

Measuring Progress

Stories

You can't be expected to keep all the assignments and projects as well as all the conversations about them in your head all the time. Make notes on your computer or in a notebook. It's the best method yet devised by time management experts.

One method you can use to measure progress on a goal is to create a planning card file for the assignment or project in a spreadsheet program or on a 3 × 5 card for each assignment. Jot down the objective, the deadline, and the results you expect from the reporter. Select dates on which to review progress. When the project is completed, note whether the goal was achieved, exceeded, partially met, delayed, or not met, and why. Copy the results to your master file on each reporter. These notes will be useful at annual performance reviews. A sample planning card appears in Figure 2.1.

Assignments

There's a lot more to newsroom management than story assignments. You may ask your people to do research, summarize an article for a sidebar, write photo captions, make phone calls, write obituaries, collect monthly reports or other data, call a source, search Web sites, or a host of other daily newsroom tasks. Some of this work may take several hours, even days, or it could involve a series of steps. For example, you may ask a reporter to search for Web sites for a story on labor trends in your area. Once found, that information must then be downloaded, typed into a format for comparison, and reviewed. Further research may be necessary after a chart is first created.

You can track progress for such assignments as well as set up a system to warn you if the goal may not be met on time by establishing milestones. Prepare a file on your computer that the reporter can access through your local area network. Rather than attempting to follow up on each assignment yourself, require the reporter to keep you informed by filling in blanks in the progress report (see Figure 2.2). A date the reporter fills in at each milestone often is enough.[3]

Because few reporters relish filling out reports, it's your responsibility to make sure each milestone is recorded when it is done. Reporters are less likely to take offense at frequent follow-up from you if you all agree in advance that this is a timesaver. A good follow-up system that also simplifies reporting is a card showing the date and time the milestone is due

22   Managing

Figure 2.1 Sample Spreadsheet Planning Card: Microsoft® Excel or Lotus 123® Spreadsheet Application

			Objectives			
		Results expected from objectives for				
Reporter Name						
Story						
Objective #1 _____						
			Results			
Review dates	Date achieved	Exceeded expectations	Partially done	Delayed (reason)	Notes	
Objective #2 _____						
			Results			
Review dates	Date achieved	Exceeded expectations	Partially done	Delayed (reason)	Notes	

Objective #3 _____

Review dates	Date achieved	Exceeded expectations	Results Partially done	Delayed (reason)	Notes

Figure 2.2 Milestone Progress Report Chart

Task	Milestone	Date Done	Reporter's Comments	Editor's Comments

and is finished, by story or by project. This system will help all of you keep current.

Put the burden on yourself to make sure deadlines are met; ultimately, that's where the burden belongs. Figure 2.3 shows a progress report with tasks, milestones, reporter's comments, and the editor's responses filled in.

One of your principal duties as editor will be assigning stories. How can you be sure you match the right reporter with the right story? In the next chapter we look at techniques to accomplish one of the most important activities you will practice as editor: distributing work.

Figure 2.3 Sample Page with Comments

Task	Milestone	Date Done	Reporter's Comments	Editor's Comments
Search Web sites for drilling statistics and list number of sites found	5/11			Try to do this today.
Sites	5/11	5/11	6 sites found	OK. Check all six and download sites with information we discussed.
Drilling statistics and reserves	5/12	5/12	6 have drilling statistics; one missing stats on reserves	Continue without five
Comparison charts	5/15	5/16	Charts prepared in Excel file. See file: oil.xls	
Charts to be reviewed by editor	5/17	5/17		Reviewed 5/17
Search for more information if requested	5/18			Get Texas production figures for #2 and get Louisiana production figures for #5
Prepare final chart	5/20	5/20	Texas done. Latest Louisiana drilling stats are being updated and will be available tomorrow.	OK 5/21

Notes

1. While an in-depth review of all management functions would be beneficial, it is not the purpose of this book. Selected aspects of management functions as they relate specifically to the editor's role are discussed in this chapter.
2. Information Technology
3. Make certain neither you nor the reporter use a date field command to write in the date, since the field will update automatically in some word processing programs each time the file is opened.

3 | Distributing Work

After you finish this chapter, you will be able to:
- Select the right reporter for the assignment, then trust that person to do it right
- Explain the purpose of the assignment and your expectations
- Understand a reporter's communication style and adapt to it to be more easily understood
- Deal with reporters who balk at assignments

Introduction

As an editor, you're responsible for the content of the editorial product you deliver to your readers, viewers, or radio audience. At a small newspaper or station the publisher or owner might be involved in editorial content, even work side by side with you reviewing content or writing editorials. But ultimately, it's your responsibility to make certain that the content meets the guidelines established by your company.

Each publication or broadcast should strive for a balanced mix of editorials. This may include (depending on the medium) hard news, photographs or video, features, columns, illustrations, live reports, investigative stories, and backgrounders. It can include specialized material such as lifestyles, business news, sports, comics, syndicated material, obituaries, and other content unique to your medium. Balancing the mix is not an easy job. To accomplish it efficiently, you will depend on your staff to deliver quality stories that require minimum editing.

This means you will assign stories to be finished within a specific time frame, usually the day of the assignment. This is generally done in a daily news conference when you plan the content for the day. Some stories will not have to be assigned. Sports reporters, for example, routinely cover certain events with little supervision. But the lead, and perhaps other stories require your personal attention. You will devote most of your time to these stories; you may even work with other editors on layout as well as how stories are played.

Much of the lead section of a newspaper or broadcast will be dictated by events. Beat reporters will suggest or submit other stories. You will assign much of the rest.

Assigning Stories

Typically, as an editor, you'll assign stories in one of four ways:

1. On a daily basis, generally during your news conference
2. During the day if a breaking story needs immediate attention
3. As new developments in a story emerge
4. At the suggestion from a reporter

You will also assign a variety of other tasks to people in your newsroom, tasks that have little to do with story assignment. See Figure 3.1.

You'll want to be confident that the most competent reporter covers each story. How can you be sure you match the right reporter with the

---

Figure 3.1 Newsroom Tasks Checklist

- ❑ Research for standing features that are published or broadcast on a daily, weekly, or monthly basis
- ❑ Text for boxes, wrap-ups, sidebars, summaries, photo captions, other non-bylined material, and occasional material such as prewritten obituaries for important persons in your area
- ❑ Telephone calls to follow up on a story
- ❑ Interviews by telephone, fax, e-mail, or personal visit to collect background or research material
- ❑ In-depth and background pieces
- ❑ Stories for supplements
- ❑ Follow-up on news tips
- ❑ Check a source, a fact, or the spelling of a name
- ❑ Year-enders

right story? Beat reporters in your newsroom already know what they need to do and are doing it, but other, less-experienced reporters may need direction or guidance on how to cover a story.

When you assign a story to an individual or a reporter to a beat, launch a column, or select a reporter for an investigative piece, you are in effect putting your trust in that person for that specific project. You expect the reporter to do the job on time every time, and to do it right. This means you must select the right individual for the job as well as communicate your expectations clearly. You can accomplish this every time you assign a story if you

- Allow enough time to thoroughly discuss the assignment with the reporter. Misunderstandings of story assignments in a newsroom are frequently caused by rushed assignments.
- Make sure the reporter understands your expectations. Misunderstandings of story assignments in a newsroom often result when a reporter misinterprets the assigning editor's information.

The Assignment Session

Begin the session by providing the reporter with any information you already have and how you envision its development. List the information you have:

- Names of people, places, or things
- Phone numbers and addresses of sources and e-mail addresses
- Web sites that may contain related information
- Stories in the morgue or other background sources
- Names of reporters, producers, photographers, or broadcast news personnel who might have worked on this in the past and can provide information or guidance
- Other sources the reporter can investigate to develop the story
- Other information you have for a specific story

Sometimes editors forget that the reporter doesn't know as much about a project as they do. For instance, you may have told others to work on this story and you want this reporter to contribute. If this is the case, be sure to discuss how this assignment is related to other work being done on the same story. Use the form in Figure 3.2 to plan your assignment.

When you make the assignment, you may suggest how you want the story handled. It's vital to make sure that the reporter understands—and

Figure 3.2 The Assignment Session

	Fill in available information below
Names of people, places or things	
Phone numbers and addresses of sources and e-mail addresses	
Web sites that may contain related information	
Stories in the morgue or other background sources	
Names of reporters, producers, photographers or broadcast news personnel who might have worked on this in the past and can provide information or guidance	
Other sources the reporter can investigate to develop the story	
Other information you have for a specific story	

retains—both your instructions and your expectations. This is not automatic: You may think you are communicating clearly with the reporter, yet he or she may interpret your instructions quite differently. A technique that will help you determine whether the reporter understood you is to ask the reporter to sum up your instructions in his or her own words. Don't expect the reporter to parrot you: "How do you plan to do this story?" is a much better question than "Did you get all that?" You'll get better results if you are efficient, focused, and avoid interruptions. The time you invest at the outset will save time later because the reporter will cover the story right the first time.

Here's an example of what can happen when a story is assigned without making sure the reporter understood the message. When I was editor-in-chief of a city magazine, I asked a reporter to do a round-up of self-serve salad bars, which were just being introduced into fast food restaurants. The objective was to explore protection from contamination by crowds of diners hovering over the food. During her interviews, the reporter discovered that desserts were offered at self-serve salad bars and that several chefs made their own ice cream in-house. That sent her off in a different direction. She spent her time researching ice cream manufacturing. Eventually, she turned in a long, well-researched piece on ice cream manufacture, pointing out that the chef at one fast-food restaurant told her that homemade ice cream tastes better. She included how ice cream is flavored and colored. Her final paragraph pointed out that, to prevent contamination, milk-based products should not be left out too long. That was not the story I had assigned. I had already commissioned art for the story and photographs were ready to illustrate a story on salad bars, not ice cream.

Understanding Communication Styles

An effective way to make sure the reporter understands what you want and what you expect is to identify with the reporter's communication style, then adapt your message to it. There are four communication styles, which fall into two broad categories:

1. Outward-oriented or extraverted
2. Inward-oriented or introverted

Try to identify one of these styles in each of the reporters you work with and do your best to adapt your message to that style to increase the chances that your message will be understood the first time. A caution: People do not fall neatly into one of these types. Usually a person will have characteristics of more than one. But one trait can be identified as predominant.

Outward-Oriented or Extroverted Styles

THE SELF-STARTER

Confident, self-assured, and opinionated, the self-starter seems to have all the answers, ranging from how best to write a story to the true, hidden motives of all the newsmakers in your community. Because these reporters are natural informal leaders with quick minds, they are often impatient with others who can't keep up with them. They are decisive; they will step in and take charge when others vacillate. Consequently, they tend to dominate their colleagues.

Self-starters are open and direct, and insist on getting immediately to the point. They can obstinately defend their ideas even when they are proven wrong. Since they are extremely competitive, they are quick to voice strong opinions about journalism and its failings, and how others should do their jobs. They instinctively grasp the fundamentals of a story and how best to handle it, and will often give advice to others even when it is not sought. This type of person will take risks, is adventurous, and will try something new. Often good editors, they tend to work best alone. More than other personality types, these are the people who help create the reputation journalists have as blunt and aggressive.

Your instructions to this individual should be brief: Present the options. When assigning a story, get to the point, avoiding detailed examples since they are generally unnecessary.

THE CHARMER

The charmer is imaginative and outgoing, and tends to exaggerate. Talkative, delightful to be with, this type often acts impulsively, so he or she may require more supervision than others. These people also need a close watch because they can be undisciplined and can let deadlines slip. They have a healthy sense of humor. Natural actors, they have a talent for the dramatic.

The charmer is emotional, changeable, and flexible. An important characteristic to keep in mind is that the charmer craves recognition. Since they are intuitive, they are able to work fast, but check their work carefully because they are also often disorganized.

Because the charmer has a strong need for recognition from others, you'll do well to acknowledge the person's contribution. You may want to present a story in terms of how it will enhance the individual's status. Get to the point quickly, but give the charmer plenty of background information. Present a broad picture when making assignments and use language that stimulates the imagination.

Inward-Oriented or Introverted Styles

THE ORGANIZER

Quiet, introspective, and cautious, this personality needs to know how all the pieces fit. When you want a systematic, slow-paced, persistent, and perfectionist reporter to cover a story, assign it to someone with this style. These reporters enjoy covering science, math, business, and engineering beats. Because they thrive on logic, they tend to analyze each story and may get bogged down trying to make sense out of seemingly illogical information. They work especially well alone. Numbers-oriented, they are probably the journalists in your newsroom most comfortable with computers, software, and spreadsheets. They're loyal, dependable, and predictable. They thrive on details and you can count on them to be thorough. They're planners; they prefer working from a schedule during their day, and will systematically and efficiently follow it. Because they are orderly, they dislike surprises or abrupt changes in their plans.

You'll get this detail-conscious reporter's attention and full cooperation most quickly by carefully planning your conversation. Include lots of facts. This reporter is especially good at stories requiring details and research. Try to be precise when you assign, providing as many details as you can. Anticipate questions during your planning before assigning a story to this person, and try to have the answers because they will have questions.

THE TEAMMATE

Team-style reporters are slow to accept change; they like things fine just as they are. Consequently, they dislike surprises, particularly in the newsroom. They are agreeable, calm, steady, trusting, open, and reliable. They have a natural skill for interviewing. They relate well to others on an emotional level: They're good team players. They find it easy to support others and you can count on them to gain support from others as well. They are not likely to spend time making contacts at cocktail parties because they avoid large groups. They will work doggedly at a story because they have a need to complete tasks. This person, who responds to the emotional angle of a story, often describes an event in terms of "how it feels." One drawback you should be aware of is that many have a tendency to remember and resent slights.

Assign stories to these individuals when you need someone who can empathize with the subject's feelings. They study a story carefully so they may be slow to act. They often like stories that will strengthen their position with others in the newsroom. Count on them to cooperate with others when you need several reporters to develop a story. A caution: Teammates find it hard to say no and willingly take on too much.

Pairing Assignments

Besides using your understanding of these styles to communicate effectively, you can try to match a story with a particular personality type.

- Pair the self-starter with a story that requires creativity, digging, and initiative.
- Pair the charmer with a story that requires convincing sources to reveal information.
- Pair the organizer with a story that requires a great deal of legwork and research.
- Pair the teammate with a story that has an emotional element.

Handling Reporters Who Balk at Assignments

Some editors tend to rely on certain reporters they know they can count on. They single out reporters who willingly accept any assignment and avoid those who grumble over extra work. But this can backfire. The following case reviews this problem. Study the case and then determine what you would do.

Case Study: Are You Picking on Me?

An editor has kept a particular reporter on the night shift in spite of occasional protests. The editor traditionally asks the reporter to work on New Year's Eve. The reporter has special skills needed for the second shift. Although the editor feels this person is the most reliable person in the department, the editor has never expressed this.

The reporter finally has had enough and asks the editor to be moved to another shift. The editor refuses. The reporter responds, "I seem to be the only person you pick for the tough jobs. I feel like you're picking on me! Don't I rate any respect around here?"

How would you respond?

Would you make the same decision as the editor in this case? If not, explain.

What do you think the real issue is here? Is the editor picking on the reporter or does the editor trust the reporter more than the editor trusts other reporters? By responding with a description of expectations, the editor can try to identify the real issue.

The response might begin, "You are the person I most trust for the second shift. I have kept you in that position because there is no supervision on that shift, and you work well without supervision. I'm confident that your work will always be of the highest quality. Now that you've heard my reasons for keeping you on the second shift, what do you think I should do?"

Whether you assign a beat, a story, a desk, or, as in this case, a shift, when dealing with resistance from reporters, try to determine whether the reporter's initial response reflects the real issue. Anger often covers up a deeper emotion. As you discuss the issue, give the reporter plenty of time to explain the problem in detail. And don't interrupt. Dennis Hamilton, a trainer and human resources consultant, says, "Typically, the last sentence they say is the most important. Employees work up to the message they want to deliver."

Following are the steps for dealing with reporters who resist an assignment.

1. Identify the real issue.
2. Restate the issue.
3. Ask for an opinion from the reporter.
4. Start your reply with a description of duties.
5. Ask the employee to help you resolve the issue.

Sometimes a task will provide the reporter with valuable experience, enjoyment, self-fulfillment, or even prestige. Reporters, producers, photographers, and broadcast news personnel are not always aware of these perks unless they are spelled out. You can reduce grumbling about extra work by describing such advantages.

Take the time to plan, assess the reporter's communication style, and anticipate resistance when you distribute work. You'll save time and reduce complaints about the work later.

As editor, you will generally hire the reporters who will work with you. The next chapter looks at techniques to interview and select applicants for positions in your newsroom.

4 Interviewing Job Applicants

After you finish this chapter, you will be able to:
- Plan each interview carefully to assure impartiality and prevent mistakes that could result in complaints or litigation
- Test the candidate's ability to produce clear, error-free, quality writing
- Explain company policies
- Understand the legal obligations of statements to reporters

Introduction

As an overworked editor in charge of a bustling newsroom, you may feel you've done enough if you briefly interview a candidate, review and verify the application, and scan a few clips to determine the candidate's ability to get the story and write it quickly and accurately. While those tasks are essential, much more is involved in choosing the right candidate.

You're more likely to find the right employee if you conduct a comprehensive interview. To comply with Equal Opportunity Employment and other federal regulations, you must also be sure that your interviewing procedure is impartial. Moreover, because newsroom personnel will work closely together in the future on ever more complex stories, you'll want to be sure the candidate will be comfortable on an investigative team.

All of this means interviews will be more time-consuming than you may like. The extra time you invest is necessary, however, to help you carry out a fair interview and avoid mistakes.

Candidates who aren't selected might challenge you. Some who have been rejected for a job may even complain to reporters in your newsroom. For example, a candidate arrived for his employment interview with jewelry pierced into different places in his face, a fashion fad at the time. He was not selected. Afterwards, he complained to someone at the company who was his friend. That worker took the rejected candidate's side and, for a while, complained that his appearance was the reason he was not hired. There were some bad feelings and camaraderie suffered for a while as a result.

Interviewing Job Applicants

Stay within Equal Employment Opportunity guidelines and affirmative action laws when interviewing a candidate. To assure you don't stray, avoid asking questions about the areas listed in Table 4.1. Note the exceptions in each case listed in the right-hand column.

Table 4.1 Problem Areas and Exceptions

Problem Area	Exception
Membership in a minority group, including race and sexual preference	Your company may have a policy of deliberately hiring a person who belongs to a minority.
Religion	No exceptions.
Marital status, family status	You can ask only when your company has a policy of asking this question of both sexes. You can also ask if the status is directly related to job qualifications.
Weight and height	Can be asked only if questions are directly related to job qualifications.
Age	No exceptions.
Commitment	You can discuss a candidate's willingness to work long hours, perhaps drop everything at home to contribute to a major breaking story.
Language	You can ask if a person is fluent in another language but not if the person learned it at home.

Recruiting Candidates

Before you can interview candidates, you'll need to recruit them. One method is to post jobs within your own organization. In a tight job market, on the other hand, you may find it necessary to run a help wanted ad. To entice top-notch candidates, your ad must make the job, the company, and the city sound attractive, a task better suited to a copywriter than an editor. However, with a little practice, you can convert a drab ad into one that accurately describes the position in terms that make the job sound exciting.

Start by writing a profile of the candidate you seek. Use a summary of this profile to advertise the position in newspapers in your area or nationally, in magazines such as *Editor & Publisher*, RTNDA *Job Bulletin*, or on the Web at Broadcast Employment Services.[1] A sample of the elements you may want to include when preparing a candidate profile appears in Table 4.2. Test your skill—fill out the one that has been left blank.

After you've prepared the profile, write your classified ad. In all cases, add Affirmative Action and Equal Opportunity Employer (AA/EOE). Preparing an ad to attract the right candidate is an art. Write each carefully. Several examples of ads you can use as models appear in Figure 4.1. Include your telephone number only if you want to receive calls or add "No phone calls please."

Table 4.2 Position/Duties/Experience and Skills Required/How to Apply

Position	Duties	Experience and Skills Required	How to Apply
Reporter	Entry level. Cover spot news. Write features. Willing to learn the ropes.	Recent graduate. Journalism degree.	Send resume, references, and your three best college clips.
Assistant City Editor	Manage the Sunday paper. Direct special projects.	Proficient in layout, headline writing, and editing. QuarkXPress.	Send resume, references, and three clips.
Assistant Managing Editor	Oversee weekly special sections.	Reporting or copy editing background. Supervisory experience preferred. Five years' experience.	Send resume, references, and three clips.

(continued)

Metro Editor	Manage the department in a manner consistent with sound editorial and management practices to ensure performance goals are attained. Responsible for the daily operation of the department. Directly manages staff in the collection, writing, editing, and layout of editorial content.	Solid news judgment. Creativity. Team-building skills.	Cover letter describing skills, strengths, and experience. Include resume and references.
Copy Desk Chief	Oversee and coordinate the desk operation with the news editor.	Enthusiastic, energetic leader. High-energy, detail-oriented.	Cover letter explaining why you're the best candidate for this position.
Copy Editor	Page designer. Edit copy for style, grammar, punctuation, captions, pagination, and layout.	Detail-oriented. Can paginate on Harris Publishing Company system. First-rate grammar skills. QuarkXPress.	Reference from an editor at current newspaper.
Editor	Staff and project supervision. Work with freelancers. Budgeting. Business planning.	Experience building teams, mentoring staff, developing new products, and directing and coordinating content and staffing within budget.	Resume that describes professional qualifications.
Designer	Coordinate with other designers, photo, graphics, and features staff.	Experience with specific design software.	Send samples of design work and resume.
Features Editor	Oversee staff of 10. Responsible for daily features, weekend entertainment magazine, and weekend special sections.	Supervisory, planning, and editing skills and innovative approaches.	Send resume, clips, or samples of feature sections.

Assignment Editor	Plan and schedule with reporters and photographers.	Excellent written, verbal, and organizational skills.	Send resume.
Assistant City Editor	Assist the city editor. Provide leadership in city editor's absence.	Editing experience a must. Must know AP stylebook.	Send resume.
Copy Editor	Edit and design news pages.	Editing skills, layout, and design skill. Macintosh and DTI software knowledge.	Send resume.
Photo Journalist	Strong work ethic and accuracy under deadline.	Minimum two years' shooting and editing for television and live truck experience.	Send resume and samples of work.
News Director	Oversee selection and assignment of news stories.	Must be superb writer and have outstanding leadership ability.	Send resume and writing samples.
News Producer	Must be able to handle change during live broadcasts.	Minimum four years' experience, excellent writing skills, and good news judgment.	College degree preferred. Send resume, tape, and cover letter.
Videographer	Familiar with broadcast television camcorder and editing equipment.	Two years' experience in a television station.	Send resume and nonreturnable tape.
Reporter	Entry-level opportunity to generate visual stories and front newscast stories live.		Send resume.

Planning the Interview

A thorough interview need not be time-consuming, one that you dread and consequently postpone. The secret to controlling the amount of time you spend with each candidate is to interview efficiently as well as effectively. And the secret to efficient interviewing is to plan your interview.

Your plan for interviews need not be elaborate, but it should be complete, so that you ask the same questions of each candidate and can make fair comparisons. This will also protect you legally.

Figure 4.1 Sample Ads

REPORTER. Aggressive, eager, entry-level reporter willing to learn the ropes in a highly competitive newspaper market. Clips must demonstrate an ability to write with flair. Send resume and best clips to Executive Editor, *Newspaper*, P.O. Box 000, Your City, State ZIP. EXECUTIVE EDITOR. *Name of Newspaper*, a paper on the coast of (name of state), seeks experienced editor who loves to coach and mentor journalists to be the best they can be and has the spirit and drive to win in our highly competitive	market. If this sounds like a position you've been waiting for, send your resume to Executive Editor, *Newspaper*, P.O. Box 000, Your City, State ZIP. EDITOR *Name of Newspaper*, a 00,000-circulation AM, is looking for a top-notch journalist to head its city desk. The successful candidate will supervise a staff of reporters, photographers, and assistant editors. We're looking for a professional who can instruct and motivate a staff with varying skills to drive them to higher levels. We need an editor who can ensure fairness and bal-	ance in news coverage. A minimum of ten years on a daily newspaper preferred. Send a resume to *Newspaper*, Address, City, State ZIP. Or e-mail to jobs@thisnewspaper.com. Applications must be received by June 1. MORNING PERSONALITY. Daily on-air personality for overnight shift and commercial production. Outstanding opportunity to gain on-air experience at a commercial radio station. Technical ability to run equipment a plus. Send resume and tape to *Station*, Address, City, State ZIP.

One way to go about planning an interview is to use a Candidate Interview Worksheet, which includes questions, responses, requirements, and notes. (See Figure 4.2.) Create a separate worksheet or page for each interview.

The worksheet has four columns. In the first column list questions you typically ask in each interview, numbered consecutively. In the second column, provide space for replies to the questions in the first column. In the third column, list the various duties, responsibilities, and tasks required of the candidate with a space for a checkmark. Check the candidate's qualifications for each responsibility as you discuss them during the interview. In the fourth column, write notes on the candidate's responses and your assessment of each response as the interview develops. When the interview ends, you'll have a written record of details, an archive that will be useful later, especially if you conduct several interviews in a single morning or day. Write out all your questions on your worksheet before you conduct your first interview, then photocopy the page.

Decide in advance how much time you will devote to each interview and stick to your schedule. Write down on the form, "Candidate Interview: Requirements and Notes," what you expect from the potential employee so you don't miss any key points if you decide to devote an

Figure 4.2 Candidate Interview Requirements and Notes

Candidate name: _____ Date: _____

Interviewer: _____

Interview result: ❏ Hired ❏ Rejected ❏ Scale (1–3)

Reason rejected: _____

	Questions	Replies	Requirements, Duties	Notes
1				
2				
3				
4				
5				
6				
7				
8				
9				
10				

afternoon to interviewing several candidates. The candidate, other reporters in the newsroom, and you will be working closely together, so determine now the type of personality you're comfortable with and look for those traits in the candidate as one set of qualifications.

If you have several attractive candidates, develop a system of numerical values to score each candidate objectively. This system will also help you compare the candidates. Keep the system simple: A scale of 1 to 3 should be adequate, such as 1 = Best Fit, 2 = Second Choice, 3 = Keep Name Active for Six Months.

Virtual Interviewing

Technology has introduced another method of interviewing and hiring: virtual interviews. Contracts, psychological testing, and sometimes even interviews and hiring can be done with computers, laptops, phones, fax, live video, and so forth. Offers are made faster and interviews are likely to be less lengthy, with decisions made sooner. You may already be searching for job candidates and their resumes at Internet sites that offer job- and resume-posting services. One thing to be aware of is that some of these Internet job seekers may have several offers. As a result, they may offer their services in a talent auction in an attempt to increase their starting salary. And as interviewing over the Net increases in popularity, keep in mind that some employees may use job offers as leverage to get more money from their current employer—including you.

Journalists are mobile, so you may have to respond quickly or risk missing out on your best candidate. Rather than call a candidate back several times, for example, you should ask an applicant to come in just once for a cluster of meetings, which may take up part or all of one day.

When screening candidates by e-mail, phone, through a Web site or perhaps even a videoconference, describe your company dress code or custom to those whom you want to interview. Candidates from one area of the country, or from another country, may not be aware of the proper dress code. Casual dress may be encouraged at one company but frowned on at another. For example, I once flew from the Midwest to San Francisco for an interview with a publisher. I arrived at the reception desk in a suit and tie, expecting the interviewer to be dressed similarly. I offhandedly asked a man lounging nearby in jeans and a plaid shirt where I could find the publisher. "I'm the publisher," he said. The next day as I was making my rounds in the building I was able to identify job candidates immediately. They arrived in suits. I was already dressed in jeans.

Controlling Turnover

Determine during the interview whether the candidate is likely to be a long-term employee. One way to determine potential longevity is to review the candidate's record of employment at previous jobs. If you see a history of job-jumping, you might suspect the candidate is switching jobs solely to move up financially or careerwise. If employment periods have been brief, ask for an explanation.

Describe the job thoroughly during the interview to make sure the candidate clearly understands your expectations. New, promising reporters can become discouraged and resign prematurely if their dreams aren't realized. Don't expect reporters to volunteer their expectations about the job: People generally only reveal their expectations when they haven't been met. It's up to you to clarify the responsibilities of the beat that the reporter will be assigned to as well as how long a reporter must have worked for you before his or her stories will get a byline, for example.

Following are three of the comments most frequently heard during exit interviews from reporters who didn't stay beyond their six-month trial periods:

"I wasn't given a beat I could do well and enjoy."
"I didn't get the raise I expected."
"It wasn't the job I thought it would be."

To prevent such disappointments on both sides, ask the candidate to describe what he or she expects from this job and to express any reservations. Avoid asking close-ended questions that can be answered with a yes or no. Instead of "Do you have any questions?" ask "What doubts do you have?" or "From the way I've described this position, how do you envision the job?" Then clarify any misconceptions and dispel doubts. A provocative question you might ask during an interview is, "Was there a time when you were asked to do something that made you feel uncomfortable?" If the answer is yes, ask what it was. Then ask, "What did you do?" By working out a clear understanding now, you'll increase the chances of getting a long-term commitment from your employees.

After a new reporter has been on the job for three or four days, set aside a half hour to meet and discover how the new employee sees the job and the company. You can also use this time to address concerns and answer questions. After three weeks, check with the new reporter again.

Company Goals

A description of your company and department goals should be an integral part of every interview. Clarify your media's role in the community. Discuss your company's mission statement. The reporter should also know about any areas that are off limits, such as language your newspaper or station won't print or broadcast, or types of stories you won't carry.

Before the interview, to make certain you have this information clear in your own mind, fill in answers to the following:

1. What are your company's objectives?

   _____

2. What are your department's specific objectives?

   _____

3. What are the reporter's objectives for this position? List specific skills and duties, including experience to help you determine them.

   _____

   Now, fill out the Interview Preparation Worksheet in Figure 4.3.

Figure 4.3 Interview Preparation Worksheet

Fill out the following information and have it ready before your first interview.

What is the job description for this position?
_____

What specific work rules should this candidate know?
_____

Define "quality writing" or "quality broadcasting."
_____

What kinds of stories does your organization prefer?
_____

What types of stories does your newspaper/station avoid carrying?
_____

How often do you want a reporter to update you on stories in progress, and how do you want the reporter to tell you?
_____

What are the specific duties to be performed?
_____

Write a thumbnail description of the supervisor (yourself or the editor) the candidate will report to. (Use an organization chart to describe the company and its leadership.)
_____
_____

What is the starting pay and what are the possibilities for raises?
_____

What is the starting skill level you expect?
_____

What are the opportunities for additional training and who will pay for it?
_____

What benefits does your organization provide:

❑ Holidays   ❑ Vacation and sick leave   ❑ Insurance
❑ Pension   ❑ 401k, IRA, savings   ❑ Other benefits

Testing the Candidate

Often, interviewers ask candidates what skills they have and accept the reply without question. You need to do more than just ask about experience or accept clips to determine the candidate's qualifications for the position. Whenever possible, test your candidate on basic journalism skills. Give the candidate a story to report and write.

Here is an example of what can happen if you hire a person based on clips alone. When I was editor of a city magazine the publisher recommended a writer who had been writing for another of his publications. I read the clips the writer submitted and was impressed by the writer's polished style. I asked him to interview a prominent local executive. The writing for the story he turned in was substantially inferior to the material in the clips. When I asked the writer to explain, he revealed that his job was to summarize articles from other publications and then produce a digest version. The implication had been that the result was his own work, when in fact it was not.

Assign a trial story, then check for deficiencies in the story the candidate turns in to you, using the form in Figure 4.4.

Anticipate Personnel Needs

There may be times when you are short-staffed, especially when there is a sudden upswing in hard news coverage, and you are unusually busy. When you have to hire someone in a hurry, you might be tempted to rush through the interview. A major cause of such rushed interviews is unrealistic assessment of long-term personnel requirements. Avoid reacting continually to sudden bursts in demand for personnel by planning for the future, estimating expected turnover and future increases in staffing needs, and identifying reliable sources for candidates.

Estimate short-term personnel needs over the next six months and long-term needs over the next year to year and a half. Because technology is changing so rapidly, you ought to regularly examine the kinds of abilities or special talents that will be required for future sections, columns, or departments to meet changing audience needs. If you anticipate requirements, your search will be more thorough and your interviews will be more relaxed and productive.

Use a form such as the one in Figure 4.5 and adapt it to your department.

46   Managing

Figure 4.4 Review Criteria for a Candidate's Sample Story

Criteria	Places in the Copy Where This Occurs	Comments
I. Writing		
Important questions left unanswered.		
Story does not follow from the lead.		
Failure to justify reason source was qualified to provide quotes.		
Story written from one interview.		
II. Quality		
Careless use of words.		
Sources not fully identified or lack sufficient knowledge or authority.		
Fuzzy writing.		
Article does not present both sides objectively.		
Writing tone is biased or favors one side.		
Confusing quotes reproduced indiscriminately.		
III. Clarity		
Superficial information when more investigation is needed.		
Poorly organized.		
Wordy writing.		
Repetitious.		
Exaggerated.		
Failure to edit before submitting.		

Figure 4.5 Personnel Needs

☐ Editors:	DEPARTMENTS	COLUMNS	DATE NEEDED
Assignment	☐ Front	Title: _____	(1) _____
City	☐ Business		
Copy	☐ Sports	Title: _____	(2) _____
	☐ Lifestyles		
☐ News Director	☐ Other _____	Title: _____	(3) _____
☐ News Producer		Title: _____	(4) _____
☐ Reporter			
☐ Videographer			
SOURCE TO MEET NEED	☐ Staff	☐ Staff	☐ Name (1) _____
	☐ Outside writer	☐ Outside writer	☐ Name (2) _____
	☐ Buy service	☐ Buy service	☐ Name (3) _____

Follow-Up

Prepare a preprinted reply postcard to respond to mail inquires and a boilerplate file in your word processor to respond to jobseekers who prospect by electronic mail. Keep track of the applicant's skills, position applied for, education, EEO class, salary expected, and other information.[2] Maintain an updated file so you will have an active list when openings occur. Keep in touch with candidates who seemed promising by sending a postcard in about a year.

    Selecting the right candidate means confirming journalistic ability, but it also means building a staff of writers who can create bylines that readers, viewers, or listeners will grow to trust and quote. That's the challenge you face with every interview. Planning and conducting a quality interview will help assure a quality team. Take the time to select the best.

48 Managing

New Hires

Explaining Company Policies

As an editor in a constantly changing newsroom, one of your key responsibilities will be to make it easier for those who report to you to do their jobs better. Clearly explaining your company's policies and mission statement will go a long way toward reducing the potential for misunderstanding and conflicts.

Generally, the human resources department in a larger organization conducts orientation sessions to acquaint the new employee with benefits, health and safety regulations, and standards. In smaller organizations, however, this task may fall on you. Yet few editors take the time with new people to review personnel policies and benefits that affect their departments. These topics, if discussed at all, are generally limited to statements such as, "Here's the company manual. Read it and let me know if you have any questions."

Even if your human resources department conducts an orientation session, as the reporter's immediate supervisor it is your obligation to make sure the reporter doesn't misunderstand or misinterpret policies. While the rules of conducting business may be spelled out in detail in the company manual, there is no guarantee that the reporter will read it from cover to cover, especially if it is lengthy. Moreover, reporters may have questions, doubts, or misinterpretations when they do read the manual. Typically, they'll consult the manual only when an issue comes up that affects them and then go directly to that topic. On top of all this, personnel policy manuals are generally handed out when a new hire is under a certain amount of first-week-on-the-job stress.

Empathizing with the Stress of a New Hire

Put yourself in the place of a new reporter during that first week on the job in your newsroom. What challenges do you think that person faces? What policies, traditions, methods, people, or places does that person need to learn about? The new reporter has to learn your work culture and how to survive within it. What is that culture? List the challenges a new reporter in your newsroom is likely to face:

_____
_____
_____
_____
_____

Now compare your list with some of the things that new reporters commonly must learn:

- New tasks
- The names and jobs of new coworkers
- Performance standards
- How to navigate the building
- Where supplies are stored and the requirements for checking them out
- New computer applications
- How to use equipment such as copiers, PCs, printers, and communication and video equipment
- How to use unfamiliar software
- Employer's priorities
- Specific deadlines
- Company personnel policies

With all this, it's not surprising that a new reporter will devote little time during his or her first weeks on the job to reading and understanding the company manual. Most firms expect an employee to read it on his or her own time. Yet company policies affect everything the employee does at work from the first day.

Therefore, the best way to ensure that new hires understand policies is to explain them (at the very least the most important ones) in an introductory session during the first three weeks of work. If you don't, you risk that the employee will

- *Read only parts of the manual.* You're taking a chance that the reporters will sincerely think that they have read and understood the entire manual when in fact they have read only those sections that attract their attention.
- *Skim the manual.* You're taking a chance that the reporter will not know about policies that directly affect your department.
- *Put the manual aside to be read some other day.* You're taking the chance the manual will never be read. This is the most common scenario. Since one of the last things on your mind during your first weeks with a new reporter is the employee manual, it's unlikely that you will be asking if there are any questions about it.
- *Interpret the manual according to experience on the job.* You're taking the chance the reporter will expect a certain kind of treatment because this was never spelled out. For example, a reporter may notice some people receiving preferential treatment, benefits, or perks, and make an assumption, which may not be vocalized. The reporter might

assume, "Charlie and Harry receive special treatment or favors, why not me?" The reporter may not know why unless policies are explained from the beginning.

Making Sure Policies Are Understood

Keep in mind that policies are guidelines. They should not be considered black and white, either/or rules for behavior. They can and should be interpreted according to circumstances, with some exceptions.[3]

To make sure the reporter understands the policies in the company manual, review the "must know" sections during the orientation session. Impress on the reporter the importance of reading the manual, but don't expect the reporter to go home and read the entire manual in one sitting, unless the manual is brief (eight pages or less.) Assign it as homework over a period of weeks.

Then meet for five minutes or so to go over one topic. You don't need to sit down at a desk or table to do this; a quick chat over a beverage may be enough. During the chat, ask the reporter to apply a section to his or her specific job. Ask the employee to describe how the material influences, modifies, or changes how he or she expects to do the job. Listen carefully to make sure that principles and standards are interpreted accurately. Clarify misinterpretations. Ask the reporter to give you a specific example if a statement is made that you think is vague or unclear.

If your company does not yet have a satisfactory personnel manual, you'll find a list of items to consider in the appendix.

Company Benefits

The best time to discuss benefits is before employment begins. Explain the medical plan. If health, dental, and disability benefits are tied to a health maintenance organization (HMO) or some other plan that limits preferences or choices, explain how to select a primary care provider and who else in the reporter's household may be eligible.

Depending on your particular company's policies, other benefits might include reimbursement for education expenses, a credit union, compensation for jury duty, bereavement pay, and holiday and vacation pay. Savings and retirement plans will also be a part of the discussion on full company benefits as well as how many years of employment are necessary before the company vests employees with full rights. Encourage reporters to save 10 percent of their income and deposit the amount in savings before depositing their paycheck.

Don't forget to describe perks such as special parking privileges for employee of the month, casual dress day, automatic paycheck deposit, a company arrangement for discounted purchase of tradeout merchandise, and other amenities that your company provides to attract and keep top people.

Make sure you describe each point clearly to prevent the employee from mistakenly interpreting company benefits that could lead to loss of pay or even disciplinary action. In one example of an erroneous interpretation, a reporter took the day off to attend his great grandfather's funeral, interpreting bereavement benefits to cover anyone in the family. Only later did he learn that the benefit was for immediate family members only and that he would not be paid.

The initial orientation session is an excellent time to give new employees an opportunity to ask questions. You can resolve any differences if the employee has misinterpreted anything. You are looking especially for any unfounded expectations. Explaining company policies helps reduce conflicts and criticism from disgruntled employees, who may later explain a disappointment with, "No one ever told me, so I just assumed this was the company policy." You can take a further precaution: Insert a form for the employee to sign, acknowledging that he or she has read the manual. This will also document that your conversation discussing the manual's contents took place. See Figure 4.6. Ask whether the reporter has finished reading the manual and signed the page. Human resources professionals suggest that you encourage employees to take advantage of the benefits your company offers since not all employees use them spontaneously.

Your Legal Obligations

Some statements you might make to reporters could be construed as promises to them. This is especially true if your company's employee handbook is considered a binding contract. Review company policies with legal counsel to determine what statements you can safely make, as well as those you should not make, to new reporters when explaining policies.

Figure 4.6 Acknowledgement

I have read and understood this manual. If I have any questions I will consult my supervisor.

Name   Date

In some states, courts have determined that your employee manual is a contract between your company and its employees, and is binding, despite any disclaimer in the manual. Manuals usually state that the handbook is only a guide, but this may not be enough. A judge could interpret the manual as a contract between the company and its employees; some courts have already ruled this way. Find out from your legal counsel if this is true in your state. If it is, your company will be obligated to deliver on any promises you make with respect to interpretation of the company manual.

If the company manual is indeed considered a binding contract in your state, then the company can't make changes without the employees' consent. In some states, you are even limited as to how and when you can revise the handbook. The most cautious approach is to consider that you will be committed to deliver on anything you offer.

Check with your legal counsel to find out just what statements you might make that could be construed as promises, especially under the terms of the handbook. For example, you might make a comment to an incoming reporter that the reporter can certainly count on a job here if he or she does well. That could be construed as a promise of job security, a promise the company might later find difficult to keep.

The responsibility to understand company policies and procedures is two-way: It is your responsibility to understand policies and where they limit you, and those who report to you should understand that policies are designed to assure a comfortable, safe, and prosperous workplace and that conforming to the policies benefits the individual as well as the team.

Now that you have your staff in place, you will want to encourage each reporter to strive to constantly do his or her best. This is accomplished with continuous motivation. It's one of the most important skills you will practice. This is easier than it sounds because reporters love to be told when they're doing a good job. In the next chapter we look at ways of motivating reporters.

Notes

1. Broadcast Employment Services, P.O. Box 4116 Oceanside, CA 92052 (Business) (760) 754-8177 (FAX) (760) 754-2115, or e-mail info@tvjobs.com.

2. Applicant Tracking/HR Tools software is available for $195 from JALMC, P.O. Box 819, Jamestown, NY 14702-0819.

3. Investigate your state's employment-at-will policy with your legal counsel, since certain promises in the manual can nullify this policy. Also, ask your attorney to review with you the pros and cons of using a "for cause" list for termi-

nation as well as electronic communication and workplace surveillance policies. With respect to illegal drug and alcohol abuse, human resources experts recommend you consider this only as it affects performance rather than as a personal problem of the employee. Be cautious: It is unwise to conclude from symptoms that a person abuses alcohol or drugs since diabetes produces some of the same symptoms. If you have reason to suspect such a problem is affecting fulfillment of employment requirements, pass the matter to your human resources director, who may refer the issue to a treatment specialist if it affects job performance. Your company's employment assistance program (EPA) may also be used for this. If you want to research alcoholism further, read Chapter 11 of *Alcoholics Anonymous*, published by Alcoholics Anonymous World Services, Inc., available in your library.

SECTION TWO

Motivating

5 | Motivating Reporters and Managing Change

After you finish this chapter, you will be able to:
- Understand the journalist's need for recognition and know how to meet it
- Understand three motivation styles to inspire reporters, improve productivity, and enhance job satisfaction
- Motivate reporters to accept change
- Deal with resistance to change and carry out change successfully

Introduction

Journalists deal with change every day in the stories they cover. Yet, as you are probably aware from your own experience as a journalist, most reporters do not manage change well in themselves, their newsroom, or in their work rules. Most need little motivation when a story energizes them. But not all stories energize. And tradition, a powerful influence, hinders change. Reporters need encouragement and not only on slow news days. Moreover, they need to accept change, which is inevitable, in spite of tradition. In this chapter we will look at both of these challenging—and related—skills: motivating reporters and managing change.

One of the strongest needs in every human being is the need for recognition and appreciation. This need is so powerful that people will go to extraordinary lengths to win attention and favor from others, especially from those with influence or in positions of authority. Reporters are less likely to strive for approval when the boss bestows it spontaneously and frequently. An important exception to this is an employee plagued by low self-esteem, not uncommon in a newsroom, who will continue to strive for approval even when compliments are frequent.

Editors ought to recognize and encourage their staff regularly, but many editors shun even the thought of praising others. "No one ever praised me," they might argue, or "Why should I praise people for doing their job?" This attitude is shortsighted. These editors fail to recognize that a compliment rates as one of the most effective and economical methods of increasing productivity and improving employee morale. It also builds loyalty. When an immediate business need arises, the editor can make a "withdrawal" from this loyalty "bank."

Compliments are unsolicited feedback from the editor acknowledging job and work approval. They can range from a simple verbal pat on the back to a "good work" note on a story. Recognition can be more formal and substantial, such as a memorandum recognizing a job well done or a bonus.

While this is often referred to as motivating people, in reality you can't actually motivate people—people motivate themselves. What you do is encourage those who report to you to become enthusiastic about their jobs and stay that way. Through inspirational leadership, you provide an ambience that encourages highly motivated and enthusiastic reporters.

Why should reporters be praised, as one recalcitrant editor put it, just for doing what's expected of them and they're paid to do? The answer is that lack of positive feedback from the boss is close to the top of any employee list of reasons for job dissatisfaction. And job dissatisfaction generates poor morale in your newsroom.

Three Motivation Styles

"I always hear about it when I mess up," a reporter complains, "but I never hear about it when I do a good job." From the reporter's point of view, encouragement is a fundamental need. Try to recall the times when your supervisor has complimented your work, as either a reporter or editor. How did you feel? Spontaneous recognition is one of the most highly appreciated, yet most underutilized management tools available to an editor. It is an especially powerful tool to motivate reporters to

- Research more thoroughly
- Cross-check more often
- Search for more stories
- Write more carefully

Several inspirational styles are available to you. Which you choose depends on the style you're most comfortable with and on the circumstances. You may need to prod your people often on a slow news day, and compliment the team less frequently when the adrenaline is flowing during a major story. The three styles for inspiring your staff are

- Leadership by example
- Cheerleading
- Spontaneous inspiration

Leadership by Example

Senior editors who are physically isolated from those who report to them, or busy editors who prefer to inspire by example, often use this method. They feel that if they work diligently the reporters will get the message and work hard, too. However, this method fails to satisfy that basic need in reporters, producers, photographers, and broadcast news personnel for recognition for their valuable work.

Cheerleading

Cheerleading practically demands you keep yourself and everyone else in a constant state of excitement and make stimulating speeches to the troops frequently. This method can be extremely effective for intense or repetitive work: round-the-clock work on a breaking story such as a plane crash, assassination or bombing, a monotonous job digging for facts, or a story that slams into dead ends from uncooperative sources. However, few editors have the time or the inclination to exhort constantly.

Spontaneous Inspiration

This style is by far the best suited to journalism. Spontaneous inspiration is brief, sincere, frequent, one-on-one encouragement, either verbally or in writing. You might say to the reporter, "Good job," or "You handled that well," or a similar compliment, or write a comment on a story you read or edit. It only takes a few seconds and you don't have to be excited all the time. Spontaneous inspiration works best when it's used selectively. Add just a dash of incentive here and another there, the way you'd flavor a dish with just a pinch of pepper. Spontaneous inspiration, delivered on a regular basis, can help you create an atmosphere that will be more amenable to change as well as help you keep resistance to it to a minimum.

There is no one "right way" to inspire. You need to be aware of the people you work with and adjust your style accordingly.

Understanding the Need for Approval

Reporters love to be told when they're doing a good job; their determination to excel expands when you notice—and tell them. Inspiration is especially beneficial to encourage reporters to be innovative, perhaps take risks. You want your people to try new ideas, to be self-starters, to come forward with suggestions rather than wait for direction from you. This involves risk. Because employees take a chance when they make decisions on their own, compliment your people immediately when they take that risk and succeed. If they fail, avoid a public reprimand or the reporters may never take another risk. Some failures, in fact, can be celebrated if they aren't fatal and the employee learns an important lesson.

Positive feedback takes interest and commitment on your part. Understanding this need does not mean you are responsible for making sure your reporters are happy and completely satisfied, but you can do your part to make their work more pleasant. Regular encouragement is a key to effective supervision and one of the fundamental differences between a boss and a leader. Recognition of the needs of each individual who reports to you is a key to effective motivation.

In all cases, the inspiration that works best is inspiration that encourages reporters to take responsibility for their own success. This means they will strive on their own to seek more and better stories, improve the quality of their writing, study texts on journalism and writing, and contribute to the influence and reputation of the company and its service. Encouraging reporters to become more highly motivated is one of the most important activities you will carry out as editor. Practice it continuously and you will contribute to developing a smooth, cooperative team. Without it you are much more likely to struggle to achieve your objectives.

Helping Reporters Manage Change

Convincing reporters they need to change and then guiding them through it can challenge your skills as a supervisor. Although *you* know that change is inevitable, the tenacity with which reporters cling to their customs when practicing journalism is legendary. But reporters are not unique; most employees resist change. Status quo reinforces a sense of security, and security is one of the primary needs in every human being. However, conventions must continually be challenged in our cyber-quick society as part of the growth process of any organization.

The types of changes that can occur sporadically in a newsroom are listed in Table 5.1

You are primarily responsible for the successful presentation of the need for change to your staff and for a smooth transition from the old to the new. To some extent, the method you use to announce change and then manage it will influence how reporters receive, accept, and adapt to it. Therefore, your success as an agent of change in your newsroom can be measured by your reporters' success in achieving it. How well you accomplish your goal depends on how well you prepare your staff for the change as well as on your leadership during the change process.

Change can impact a reporter, sometimes profoundly, and can show up in such areas as mental health and life at home. But when thought out carefully, and planned and managed successfully, change can develop smoothly into the new order. Accordingly, it's important for you as a supervisor to have a procedure for helping reporters deal with change. This procedure must be an essential element of any overall plan to implement change.

The Consequences of Change

Before we review a procedure for managing change, let's take a moment to reflect on the consequences that could result if change is not handled properly. Problems can arise in two areas: difficulties that affect the newsroom and difficulties that affect the reporter.

Change can cause anxiety in personnel if not managed appropriately. In Table 5.2, next to each change listed on the left, write in the middle column the anxiety you think might result from the change; and in the

Table 5.1 Changes That Can Occur Sporadically in a Newsroom

1. A promotion	5. Changes in page makeup
2. New office or building	6. New responsibilities
3. New editor, reporter, columnist, or intern	7. New technology
4. New beat or task	8. Changes in company ownership

Table 5.2 Typical Changes in a Newsroom

Changes	Anxiety That Might Result from Change	Consequences of Improperly Managed Change in a Newsroom
Reassignment to a different job		
New editor, reporter, or intern		
Different beat		
Changes in section		
New responsibilities		
New technology		

right-hand column write the adverse consequences you think might result if change is not managed properly. When you finish, match your thoughts against the suggested list in Figure 5.1 at the end of this chapter.

Types of Changes

Let's look at examples of changes you may be called on to implement and how poor preparation can affect your newsroom as well as reporters.

New or Modified Company Regulations

Top management frequently communicates changes in company rules with a memo. Often, management fails to provide background or to explain the change. This is strange behavior coming from media management. Reporters are expected to provide background for every story, yet senior media executives regularly fail to provide an explanation (or background) when they announce a change. Reporters who are not told the reasons for modifications in company rules, regulations, procedures, or customs may interpret the changes as criticism of their work or worse, interference with it.

Restructuring

Restructuring generally is a synonym for *layoffs*. If the benefits to your organization are not thoroughly explained, such as increased competitiveness, improved market position, or other advantages, then insecurity—with consequent damage to productivity—may be a consequence.

Physical Changes in the Newsroom

Reporters may subconsciously associate the physical location of desks, furniture, computers, and printers with stability, strength, and permanence. Predictability reinforces the reporter's sense of belonging, one of the fundamental needs of human beings. People arriving for work expect to find their workplace—tools, equipment, papers, and locked desks—in the same place they left them the night before. Assignment to a different workstation or an unannounced rearrangement of the workspace is unsettling. A reporter will readily use another computer if he or she made the decision. This could happen if the reporter's computer crashes, for example.[1] But when forced to do so, the reporter might resist the reassignment, however temporary.

Promotions, Transfers, and Reassignments

Because of their innate competitiveness, reporters can react to the promotion of a colleague with envy, rivalry, and disappointment if they suspect the promotion was not based on merit. Promotions should come after a reporter has clearly earned it.

Technology

Improved technology often implies changes in work methods, procedures, or tools. Word processing, for example, was resisted by a generation of reporters accustomed to typewriters. Improved technology frequently imposes intellectual challenge as well as changes in work methods, especially for older reporters.

Improvements in technology often spark

- Fear of lower income
- Fear that the new tools will replace the individual
- Fear of lack of competence to master the new technology
- Fear of looking foolish in front of coworkers during training or initial use
- Fear of demotion or transfer
- Fear of supervision by younger colleagues who are comfortable with the new technology

Some fears are unfounded. When growth demands a redesigned office or a redesigned space layout in a new building, for example, reporters may fear losing the prestige, comfort, or perks of their present workspace; they may assume the new space arrangements imply inferior status. They might resist change just because they will lose the companionship and familiarity of faces of friends nearby, or an easy rapport with an understanding editor whose office was near the reporter's desk.

A certain amount of unhealthy stress can lurk in the background even for those employees who, at least outwardly, seem to welcome change and manage it successfully. Poor stress management may be today's number one cause of errors affecting newsroom quality. Serene workers make fewer mistakes. Helping your reporters deal effectively with change can reduce a reporter's resistance to change.

Resistance to Change

Here are four major ways management can trigger reporters' resistance to change:

1. Failure to inform reporters about the change in a timely manner
2. Failure to include reporters in the planning process
3. Failure to explain the benefits of the change
4. Failure to implement the change soon after it's announced

First, we'll review these four principal causes of resistance, and their consequences, when you or your organization implement change. Then we'll look at what you can do to avoid those problems.

1. *Failure to inform reporters about the change.* When change is carried out without warning, employees may dream up scenarios of their own to explain the change. False assumptions and rumors can create an erroneous interpretation of the purpose of the change that will be difficult to correct.

2. *Failure to include reporters in the planning process.* Reporters often resist change simply because they have not been invited to share in formulating it. Changes are difficult enough when those affected by the change are involved in making the choice; it's even more strenuous when change is imposed on them.
3. *Failure to explain the benefits of the change.* Employees may speculate on the impact the change will have on their jobs, positions, future, benefits, and even usefulness to the organization. That speculation is more likely to be negative if the value of the change to the organization is not explained.
4. *Failure to implement the change soon after it's announced.* Delay in carrying out a change, for whatever reason, creates anxiety, apprehension, and conjecture. Those who are informal leaders in your newsroom (individuals who wield influence and sway opinion) can come up with all sorts of specious explanations for the delay. Those explanations can quickly become "facts," with serious consequences when the change is finally carried out.

Remedies for Resistance to Change

FAILURE TO INFORM REPORTERS ABOUT THE CHANGE

SOURCE OF DIFFICULTY.   In your administrative role, you may become so caught up in planning for a change and its timing that you fail to consider communicating that change to reporters. You may focus so much on making sure you don't miss any of the steps in the process for the change that you overlook one of the principal steps in that process: informing the staff.

REMEDY.   Include staff communication in your plans. This sounds obvious but it is often overlooked. Decide when to inform reporters and how. For example, you may want to meet first with your entire department, then meet with individuals whom you expect will be troubled. Or you may talk to the informal leaders first to gain their support and prevent speculation.

ACTION STEP.   Develop a specific plan to communicate change to your staff and incorporate it into the planning process. As follow-up, supply documents to create a sense of security.

FAILURE TO INCLUDE REPORTERS IN THE PLANNING PROCESS

SOURCE OF DIFFICULTY.   Some editors think in terms of all or nothing when they consider asking reporters to contribute input about change. Management may feel, with a certain sense of superiority, that only a few reporters have enough experience, intelligence, or knowledge to offer worthy ideas. As a result, they involve no one.

REMEDY.   Management's attempt to find creative solutions to deal with change or growth is a delicate balancing act. During management's decision-making process, reporters are often considered the target of a management decision rather than an element of it. Balance is best achieved when reporters are involved in the decision-making process because participation generates "ownership" of the process as well as the outcome. Ownership of decisions that affect jobs is a powerful on-the-job motivator because it helps reinforce a sense of security. Reporters will make a special effort to assure "their" decisions are carried out. They will "own" the job, the team, and the future of both.

ACTION STEP.   Develop that sense of ownership by inviting staff input during the planning stage. Reporters can be involved in any aspect of planning, and at any level. Their input does not necessarily require that their suggestions be adopted. Explain at the outset all suggestions will be considered and that the best will be selected. Your people will point with pride later to any input they contributed to the final plan.

FAILURE TO EXPLAIN THE BENEFITS OF THE CHANGE

SOURCE OF DIFFICULTY.   Management decisions can be motivated by economic reasons such as

- Reaction to competition
- Opportunities in the marketplace
- Changes in management of the publication or station or Web site
- Changes in ownership
- Consolidation
- Acquisitions
- Modernization
- Personnel cuts to reduce costs
- Cutbacks due to decreased advertiser support
- Other reasons specific to your media

In all these instances, survival of the company as well as protection of jobs is the driving force. Typically, management shuns any public discussion of such issues to avoid creating an atmosphere of insecurity, protect information from competitors, and avoid generating doubts in the marketplace about the stability of the business.

REMEDY.   Progressive leaders explain the why of an action as well as the what. Unfortunately, management may erroneously conclude that revealing anything means revealing everything. This simply does not follow. Communication does not imply confession. The information that you choose to reveal can be selective.

ACTION STEP.   Share with your reporters the reasons for a change and how you expect them to carry it out. Make them a part of the process. Provide thorough explanations that motivate by recognizing the importance of the reporter.

FAILURE TO IMPLEMENT THE CHANGE SOON AFTER IT'S ANNOUNCED

SOURCE OF DIFFICULTY.   Delays are most frequently caused by either poor planning or failure of one or more elements or events to occur as expected. Often the very people assigned to effect a change may be those who cause the delay. When managers discover the cause of the delay, they might thoughtlessly blame a department or an individual. This reaction before reflection can cause internal strife and resentment.

REMEDY.   Once the change has been announced, it should be carried out immediately and according to plan. If delays occur, communicate frankly with everyone involved with as much detail as appropriate.

ACTION STEP.   Rather than focusing on the cause of the delay, focus on resolving it. Spend your time searching for solutions rather than scapegoats.

The I To U Method of Communicating Change

The *I To U* method involves communicating with the individual, team, and unit, in that order. The I To U method of communicating change helps you head off rumor and speculation while encouraging a positive attitude and commitment.

Individual

Employees want to know how they will be affected by the change. Discuss the change with the affected individuals first. Point out how the change will benefit them personally. For example, describe how a new technology can improve potential for promotion or increased wages, or explain how the change will reduce costs and protect their wages.

Team

Once their concerns about the impact the change will have on them is satisfied, reporters will be ready to listen to how their team benefits. Explain how the entire group will work more comfortably or efficiently. Make sure they understand that everyone in the newsroom is a member of the team that produces the news report.

Unit

The unit is the organization: the corporation, publication, or station. After the individual and team benefits are made clear, reporters will more willingly listen to the benefits to their company. Point out the value of the changes to the organization as a whole. These can be economic, prestigious, defensive, opportunistic, or other benefits, depending on the change. Include comprehensive information on what will remain the same as part of any meeting on change. You want to be sure employees leave with an understanding of how the changes enhance the organization's stability.

As part of this process, be open to any comments. Allow employees to express concerns, fears, resistance, opinions, and suggestions. Expect emotional reactions—they are part of the process.

If only a few employees will be affected, recognize their concerns if they bring them up during your meeting. Point out that while you recognize there may be fallout or consequences, neither you nor management are able to prepare for every eventuality. Ask the reporters, producers, photographers, or broadcast news personnel for cooperation and feedback as the change is implemented so that you can help them achieve a smooth transition.

Change Imposed by Senior Management

Let's look at an instance of change mandated by upper management without input from those it would affect. This is a true story of a situation in which the reporters were not consulted prior to implementing a change.

When information systems were first being introduced into newspapers, management at one newspaper invested a considerable amount in new computers to convert from using typewriters, redesigned the newsroom, painted the walls, and installed new carpeting. All of this was done without discussing the change with the reporters. The expensive investment in the newsroom environment was done as much to protect the investment in the equipment as it was to encourage the reporters to accept the new system and the radically different atmosphere essential to working in it. Gone were the cigars and coffee cups and food, all too dangerous for the delicate computer keypads.

The reporters refused to use the new equipment. They continued writing with typewriters.

Teams of trouble-shooting consultants were called in. They changed the color of the walls and carpeting, and even permitted food and drink at the terminals. That didn't solve the problem.

Finally, it occurred to one of the trouble-shooters to ask a reporter why he preferred to continue using a typewriter when the new computers were so much easier to use. The reporter replied that the tap-tap sound of the typewriter was gone, replaced by the terminal's silent keypad. The manufacturer redesigned the keypad to make a clacking sound when keys were touched. Soon, the reporters were busy at work at their new terminals.

This is an excellent example of the lesson management learned by attempting to impose radical change from the top without input from those it would affect.

Managing Intense Resistance to Change

You might want to consider implementing a change in stages if you meet fierce resistance, or you might test the change for a period (if practical) and then evaluate the reaction to it. After the trial, assess progress, ask for comments and suggestions, and incorporate those that are useful. This gives reporters a chance to participate in the change as they get used to it.

Other methods of managing intense resistance include

- Conducting informal conversations in the lunchroom or in your office. Talk about the problems that the change you envision will help solve, without mentioning the planned change. Try to determine if reporters are even aware of the problem that the change will correct.
- Inviting participation in a brainstorming session with the staff to review alternatives. Call the group to an informal discussion and describe the problem. Allow members of the group to spontaneously offer recommendations. But refrain from overtly asking for them: allow the group to take ownership of the need for a solution to the problem.
- Asking those who resist to explain their reasons or to suggest alternative solutions. Listen to opposing views carefully. These may well be the people who might sabotage the change if they are not convinced it is essential. Ask them why they oppose the change or why they don't seem convinced the problem needs correcting. This can help you incorporate additional measures you weren't aware of that will ensure acceptance.
- Requesting written anonymous comments. Sometimes resistance is so fierce that you have to accept that open discussion is leading nowhere. In other cases, people who generally resist change will remain silent

in meetings on the subject. One way to overcome this is to offer an opportunity for anonymous input. Anonymous suggestions can be typed and left in a suggestion box set aside for this purpose.

Managing Stress During Change

Pressure on reporters, and yourself, to meet a deadline for change can generate unhealthy stress, especially if reporters take longer to carry out or accept the change than you planned on. Here's a remarkably simple yet immensely effective technique you can use to reduce pressure on yourself in an already stressful situation: When planning change, write down your expectations. Then lower them.

First, make your plan for an ideal transition to the new procedure, and the time it will take. Then add extra time and assume that some things will go wrong. Plan for problems and slow implementation at the outset as reporters adjust. When you lower your expectations, you lower stress. The payoff: You'll be delighted with how well things are going rather than impatient and wondering why they are not going better.

Change must be carefully managed to be successful. Editors who fail to plan their changes very often are forced to change their plans. If you don't manage change according to a carefully designed strategy, you may spend more time putting out fires than implementing the new order. You can easily avoid the consequences of poorly managed change by creating a step-by-step blueprint, then communicating openly to gain commitment and acceptance. Use Form 5.1 as a planning worksheet.

Managing Follow-Up to Assure Success

You have begun to implement the change after planning it carefully and soliciting input from those who will be affected by it. Maybe you've incorporated a suggestion or two. You're not through yet because three elements are required for successful change:

1. Communication
2. Implementation
3. Follow-up

Along with monitoring the impact of the new procedure on productivity and costs, you will need to monitor its effects on the people carrying it out. Watch for signs of strain, regression, forgetting new requirements, confusion, anger as a way of dealing with fear of change, or doing things both the old and the new ways.

Form 5.1 Change Management Worksheet

1. List possible consequences in your newsroom that might result from change.

   a. _____   c. _____

   b. _____   d. _____

2. Write a plan to communicate the change to your staff.

   _____

   _____

   _____

   _____

3. Apply the I To U method of communicating the change.

   List benefits to the individuals.

   _____

   List benefits to the team.

   _____

   List benefits to the unit (organization).

   _____

4. Decide when you will inform reporters, and how.

   _____

   _____

   (Consider holding a brainstorming session to review the planned change and consider alternatives if you expect resistance.)

5. Decide at what stage you will bring the reporters into the decision-making process.

   _____

   a. When will you meet with your staff? _____

   b. How will you meet with reporters?

   ❏ Meet with entire newsroom staff

   ❏ Meet with individual reporters

   ❏ Meet with informal leaders

(continued)

(continued)

6. Meeting notes: Concerns, fears, resistance, opinions, and suggestions that were brought up during the meeting with the staff.

   _____

   _____

   _____

   _____

   Will you request written (anonymous) comments?

   ❏ Yes   ❏ No

   Method to receive comments.

   _____

7. Milestones:

   ❏ Date _____ Compliment the people who are effecting the change.

   ❏ Date _____ Compliment the people who are effecting the change.

   ❏ Date _____ Compliment the people who are effecting the change.

   ❏ Date _____ Compliment the people who are effecting the change.

   ❏ Date _____ Announce the success of the change.

Monitoring the change process will be easier if you involved the reporters in the planning stage because you shifted part of the responsibility for the success of the change to the reporters who must make it happen. This will help reduce the time and attention you need to spend monitoring the impact on the reporters. As for those informal leaders who wield influence in your department, take advantage of their role. Delegate some accountability to them and charge them with reporting any signs of difficulties to you. This is an effective method of gaining their cooperation rather than their competition.

Make sure those involved are aware that their efforts to carry out the change are noticed and appreciated. Provide positive reinforcement such as administrative support and compliments. If you have planned a change that will take some time, establish milestones to mark progress. Milestones will help you identify pitfalls to watch out for as well as successes to celebrate along the way. This gives you opportunities to congratulate the individual or the team on their efforts as well as motivate them to continue if the change is difficult.

Try to avoid focusing exclusively on mistakes or delays. Be sure to stress what's being done right, however imperfectly. Such recognition of progress builds self-confidence, eases the transition, reduces resistance, and increases motivation during the process. It will also encourage cooperation when your reporters are called on to embrace change in the future.

It won't hurt to point out any career-enhancing benefits of the change for each reporter, whether the benefits are small or large. One key to successful change is a staff that knows its supervisor is constantly seeking opportunities to enhance their career growth.

Although managing change is a not an easily acquired skill, it must be practiced to achieve proficiency. Don't treat this skill lightly simply because you don't have any changes planned right now. Change may not be contemplated today but it certainly will be part of your future.

People will respond to your leadership when you give them a clear sense of purpose and goals. They will appreciate that you treat them as individuals rather than as workers. They need to be invited to participate and contribute. They will respond—and they will respect you—when you inspire and challenge them. Above all, they will value trustworthiness. They will expect you to earn their trust by demonstrating integrity and competence.

You are more likely to inspire those you lead if you show a sincere concern for those who report to you, respect their points of view, never abuse your power, never distance yourself from those you lead, and are always available to listen.

An editor is always a boss, but a boss is not necessarily a leader. The difference between a boss and a leader is the difference between encouraging and commanding, between telling and impelling.[2] Confident leaders motivate the people who report to them to motivate themselves, then let go and watch them respond.

Meetings are a particularly useful time to encourage and inspire reporters. Make each meeting doubly effective by conveying information and inspiring reporters at the same time. This especially efficient method can generate enthusiasm as well as enhance your leadership. To be convincing and generate enthusiasm in your presentations to small groups, however, you'll need to practice principles of public speaking. In the next chapter we look at methods to increase your confidence and effectiveness as a public speaker.

Notes

1. In one instance when I was business editor of a daily newspaper, a reporter was working on a deadline when his computer crashed. He was told to use the only free computer, in the IT department. He huffed off, lugging notes, files, and clips, making it blatantly apparent that he fiercely resented the change.
2. When is a leader best? When he's practically invisible.
   A leader is poor when people obey and glorify him
   A leader is bad when people detest him.
   The best leader is one who doesn't talk much, gets his work done, and achieves his goals.
   Then, his people will say, "We did it."
   —Lao-tze, China, 6th Century B.C.

Figure 5.1 Suggested List of Anxieties and Consequences of an Improperly Managed Change

CHANGES	ANXIETY THAT MIGHT RESULT FROM CHANGE	CONSEQUENCES OF IMPROPERLY MANAGED CHANGE IN A NEWSROOM
Reassignment to a different job	Concern about job security and competence to handle different position	Possible resistance to change resulting in higher turnover
New editor, reporter, or columnist	Concern about security in the company and income	Lower morale
Different beat	Concern about career and future in company	Diminished productivity
Changes in section	Confidence to manage new format or stories	Resistance to change and strained job satisfaction
New responsibilities	Concern about competence to handle new responsibilities	Unhealthy stress
New technology	Concern about ability to understand and use new technology	Decreased cooperation

6 | Making Presentations to Groups

After you finish this chapter, you will be able to:
- Plan a presentation to your staff
- Write the presentation
- Deliver a presentation that maintains interest and achieves your objective
- Use presentations to motivate as well as inform reporters

Introduction

Good presentations are not spontaneous; they're planned. They're the result of thoughtful consideration of the content and audience, and rehearsal. Yes, rehearsal, even when you're only speaking to colleagues. Successful editors are leaders who know that well-planned presentations are opportunities to motivate as well as to inform. Superb presentations enhance your leadership. They also help you polish a critical skill you must have to advance in your career: ease as a public speaker. Your presentations—whether you speak to one reporter or 100—will have a greater impact and produce more useful results if you take the time to follow the three keys of a successful presentation: prepare, practice, and present.

In spite of the importance of preparation, many editors prefer to wing it when making presentations. Perhaps because of time constraints, they wait for a slack period in a busy day, then try to squeeze an unrehearsed talk into it. Is this your style? Or perhaps you'd just rather not stand in front of a group at all. Some editors prefer to talk to reporters one at a time, for example, rather than gather them for a meeting to discuss story opportunities or problems, or to congratulate and motivate.

Figure 6.1 What Do You Want to Accomplish?

- ❏ Train
- ❏ Persuade
- ❏ Motivate
- ❏ Instruct
- ❏ Explain
- ❏ Remind
- ❏ Introduce
- ❏ Clarify

Figure 6.2 Select the Audio-Visual Equipment You Will Need

- ❏ Overhead projector
- ❏ Slide projector
- ❏ Screen
- ❏ Pointer
- ❏ Flip chart
- ❏ Chalkboard and markers
- ❏ PC or laptop and projector
- ❏ Other electronic device

Organize Your Presentation

An organized presentation includes a beginning, a middle (or main part), and a summary. Write a sentence that summarizes and introduces your topic:

Next, jot down a quick outline of the points you will cover. The outline need not be elaborate; you're the only one who will see it. Determine whether you will need audio-visual equipment. (See Figure 6.2.)

- A flip chart is ideal for outlining and explaining points to groups smaller than ten.
- If you expect more than ten people and you will refer to printed copy, photocopy the material to an overhead transparency.
- For large groups, prepare a presentation you can project from a laptop or desktop unit to make viewing easier throughout the room.

Finally, prepare a closing statement. This statement should summarize your remarks and refer to your introductory statement to tie the presentation together.

Use the worksheet in Figure 6.3 to prepare your presentation.

Consider Your Audience

Write answers to the following questions.

Who will be in the room?

_____

_____

Which reporters will have questions?

_____

_____

Anticipate reporters' questions and plan your replies. By anticipating audience response, you can plan for extra discussion time if needed.

Question: _____

Reply: _____

Question: _____

Reply: _____

Question: _____

Reply: _____

Question: _____

Reply: _____

List the reporters who might need a more detailed explanation:

_____

_____

List the reporters who are likely to be bored:

_____

_____

_____

_____

List the reporters who will want to object, or debate, or insist on voicing their viewpoint:

_____

_____

Highlight Key Points

Determine your key points and make a note next to them in your outline so you will remember to emphasize them.

Key points:

1. _____

2. _____

3. _____

Rehearse the Presentation

Practice the entire presentation out loud several times before speaking to your audience. Rehearsal helps you become familiar with the material, which results in a smoother and more confident delivery. Rehearse your presentation as though you were presenting it. Pretend your audience is in front of you. Put transparencies on the overhead or write on the flip chart. You'll become familiar with the material and find out whether you need to make any changes. This dry run will also increase your confidence and professional delivery.

Time the Presentation

Time your delivery as you run through the presentation: Jot down the time in minutes. On the second practice run, your time should be significantly shorter. If you practice a third time, you will shorten the presentation by at least 20 percent compared with the first rehearsal. At the start of your presentation, tell your audience how long you expect to speak. It's a nice touch and helps maintain interest. Most presentations should not last longer than 30 minutes.

Vary the Presentation

Even when an audience is interested, attention wanes. We talk at about 100 to 150 words a minute, but typically we can receive information at somewhere between 500 and 700 words a minute. As a result, your audience can follow everything you say and still have time to think about other things.

Figure 6.3 Presentation Worksheet

Title _____

Purpose:

- ❏ Train
- ❏ Motivate
- ❏ Discipline
- ❏ Remind
- ❏ Persuade
- ❏ Instruct
- ❏ Explain
- ❏ Introduce
- ❏ Other _____

Objective _____

Opening Statement

_____

_____

Outline

First Key Point:

_____

Supporting Points _____

_____

_____

Second Key Point:

_____

Supporting Points _____

_____

_____

Third Key Point:

_____

Supporting Points _____

_____

_____

(continued)

(continued)

Closing Statement _____
_____

Timing

First Key Point: _____ minutes

Second Key Point: _____ minutes

Third Key Point: _____ minutes

Total: _____ minutes

Audience Composition _____

Audience Size _____

Special individuals I need to prepare for:

Name: _____   Characteristics _____

Name: _____   Characteristics _____

Name: _____   Characteristics _____

Questions:

Question _____

Answer _____

Question _____

Answer _____

Question _____

Answer _____

Question _____

Answer _____

Question _____

Answer _____

Time of first practice session: _____ minutes

Time of second practice session: _____ minutes

Maintaining Audience Interest

To keep your audience attentive, incorporate the following in your presentation.

1. Change your position. Walk from one side of the room to the other occasionally. Stand closer to your audience, but don't pace back and forth; it distracts people.
2. Encourage participation. For example, ask whether anyone has any questions. After you ask the audience for questions, give them plenty of time to respond. Silence does not necessarily mean an audience understands everything. An audience needs to hear your request, reflect on it, then determine if everything is clear, and only then think of a question. All this takes time. Stand and wait.
3. Maintain eye contact. Here's an effective method for maintaining eye contact I observed when I attended an address by a president of a country. Select a person on the left side of the room and speak directly to that person for a minute or so. Then do the same thing with a person in the middle. Now, select someone on the right side of the room. Then speak to someone at the back of the room. Repeat this technique throughout.
4. Use an overhead projector. When you turn on the projector, the sudden bright light attracts your audience's attention and creates anticipation. But don't keep the projector on for long periods; after a while the bright light annoys people.
5. Prepare handouts. A handout need not be more elaborate than a hand-written page. You don't need to prepare flashy handouts with your desktop publisher or presentation software, unless you need to explain complicated concepts. If your handwriting is hard to read, type your notes. Your audience can write on the handout, so don't forget to allow space on the page for those notes.

If you make use of all of these methods in every presentation, you'll be assured of involving three learning types: auditory, visual, and kinetic.

The Five Elements of a Successful Presentation

If making a presentation before an audience, even the group you work with every day, makes you nervous, you're not alone. Americans fear speaking in public more than anything else. However, those jitters will leave you after a few presentations; confidence increases with experience. After a few talks before your coworkers you'll forget your nervousness and begin focusing on improving your delivery and the quality of your presentation.

Once you have achieved confidence in your skill as a presenter, and nervousness has disappeared, begin working on improving each presentation. The five characteristics you should strive for are listed in Table 6.2.

Table 6.2 The Five Elements of a Successful Presentation

1.	Desire	You sincerely want to make an effective presentation.
2.	Preparation	Your presentation sticks to the point, maintains interest, and begins and ends on time.
3.	Enthusiasm	You put zest into your presentation. You make your topic, and yourself, interesting.
4.	Conviction	You are convinced that what you have to say is important and convey that. If you truly believe in what you are saying, the audience will, too.
5.	Practice	Practice produces confidence.

Sample Topics

Besides issues that specifically concern you in your newsroom, some topics are of interest to almost all reporters. The following topics lend themselves to training presentations, and some may even lead to lively debates.

1. Your company's values (or culture)
2. Responsible journalism
3. Responsibilities to the community
4. The importance of continuing education in the field of journalism
5. The changing role of journalism in our society
6. Ethical journalism

A Sample Presentation

The Ten Commandments of Ethical Journalism (see Figure 6.4) is an excellent topic for a training presentation. This list has generated stimulating discussion in seminars I have conducted for midcareer journalists. It offers you a chance to reinforce respect for and adherence to ethical journalism. Copy the list and distribute it to your group for reference during your presentation. Allow space in the margins for those who want to take notes.

Figure 6.4 The Ten Commandments of Ethical Journalism

1. Thou shalt always present all sides of a controversy.
2. Thou shalt never use your position to destroy someone.
3. Thou shalt always consider your publication or station a channel of communication and information and not a soapbox.
4. Thou shalt always faithfully reproduce quotes to precisely reflect the intent of the speaker.
5. Thou shalt always be impartial.
6. Thou shalt never accept a favor or gratuity from any source in exchange for a story.
7. Thou shalt always treat information as confidential until it appears in print.
8. Thou shalt never publish a story as a favor when it has no redeeming news value.
9. Thou shalt never charge to publish a story nor pay for one.
10. Thou shalt never interview a person if you have no intention of writing and publishing a story.

The sample presentation worksheet in Figure 6.5 has been completed for you, except for the last three lines. Fill in the names of the participants there and the reaction you expect from them. Then, based on your own experience as a journalist, and your experience with this team of reporters, write down questions or disagreement you might expect. For example, "Thou shalt never charge to publish a story, nor pay for one" may generate a discussion of television programs that pay participants for interviews. Prepare your position on this point and explain why your company does not pay sources (or why it does). Before you present this information, ask your audience to explain why sources should or should not be paid for interviews.

Successful supervision is not always easy to attain and problems will challenge you that don't seem to have an easy solution. In the next chapter we will review methods you can use for problem solving and decision making.

Figure 6.5 Sample Presentation Worksheet

Title *The Ten Commandments of Ethical Journalism*

Purpose:

- ☑ Train
- ☐ Persuade
- ☐ Motivate
- ☐ Instruct
- ☐ Clarify
- ☐ Explain
- ☐ Remind
- ☐ Introduce
- ☐ Other _____

Objective *To review my department's standards of ethical journalism with those who report to me.*

Opening Statement

You have before you this company's ten-point code of conduct, which you are expected to adhere to as long as you work here. We will discuss each point in a roundtable. Your colleagues may well contribute valuable suggestions during our discussion. I welcome your comments, ancedotes, war stories, even disagreement.

Outline

First Key Point: *These points establish a code of conduct for every reporter in this newsroom.*

Supporting Points *We expect you to memorize this list and adhere to it strictly.*

Second Key Point: *If you have difficulty understanding any of these points, or if you disagree with any of them, now is the time to state your position.*

Supporting Points *Once we have finished discussing these points, and you understand them, you will be expected to follow them without exception.*

Third Key Point: *We will review each point and I will illustrate with examples. I welcome examples, questions, or doubts you may have on any point.*

Supporting Points *Tell me which part of this presentation that you do not understand regarding the standards of ethics of this company so that I can present it in another way. Let's begin with point number one: Thou shalt always present all sides of a controversy. What do you understand that to mean?*

Making Presentations to Groups   87

Closing Statement: _We have discussed each of these points. You have expressed your opinions and we have discussed them. You now understand this company's standard of ethics, and you are expected to adhere to them exactly. Thanks for your attention and input. I want you to succeed here as ethical journalists above reproach. These principles will help you achieve that._

Timing

First Key Point: _2_ minutes

Second Key Point: _2_ minutes

Third Key Point: _4–6_ minutes

Total: _8–10_ minutes

Audience Composition _____

Audience Size _____

Special individuals I need to prepare for _____

SECTION THREE

Mediating

7 Problem Solving and Decision Making

After you finish this chapter, you will be able to:
- Use a five-step process to analyze any newsroom problem
- Know how to identify the right problem
- Select the right solution from a variety of alternatives
- Follow up effectively to assure the success of your solution

Introduction

Many editors run into difficulty with problem solving because they view the procedure itself as difficult or complex. It shouldn't be. As journalists, editors solve problems all the time; finding and accessing information, conducting interviews successfully, and writing a complicated lead are just some examples. Why, then, do editors as managers run into difficulty when attempting to solve problems when as journalists they seem to breeze through them? Here are four reasons:

- Editors aren't aware their journalism training has prepared them to solve management problems.
- Editors tend to ignore small problems.
- Editors tend to postpone dealing with any problem not directly associated with journalism.
- Editors can be overwhelmed when problems escalate.

As manager of a busy newsroom, you can handle everyday problems more efficiently and make the right decision more quickly if you take a few moments to investigate the cause of a problem before acting. You can also make your task easier if you use a step-by-step problem-solving and decision-making model. A quick review of the principles of problem analysis is a good place to start.

As a general rule, a problem is a deviation from a norm. Your first step in problem solving, then, is to determine what the norm, or standard, is. Then compare the problem with the standard to determine how the problem deviates from it. A standard is a given set of predictable circumstances, events that can be expected. So when a problem comes up, either a condition evolved that was unexpected or some part of the normal process failed to occur.

Except in an emergency, try to avoid shoot-from-the-hip decisions until you can investigate the cause of the problem. Gathering all the facts before making a decision is essential, of course. But just as important, you could miss deeper, underlying issues if you act too soon and seize the first solution that comes to mind. This is especially true if the same or a similar problem comes up often. If you take the time to compare the problem with the norm, for example, you may discover that the procedure (the norm) itself contributed to the problem, and needs to be examined and possibly modified.

For example, if a reporter is the cause of the problem, you may learn that the reporter lacks sufficient training or wasn't informed about certain rules, or you may discover that a reporter has lost motivation or interest. Such underlying information would tell you that procedures for training or recognition may need adjustment.

Steps in Problem Solving

Whether you're dealing with people, technology, or procedures, your first course of action is to review the events that led to the problem. As you investigate, make notes so that you can write a brief report. This will provide documentation in case your decision is ever challenged. Moreover, you'll have an accurate record of the statements made by those you interviewed during your investigation if you need to consult them later.

Following is a step-by-step procedure for solving a problem. As you become comfortable with it, you will be able to apply this method to any newsroom issue.

Analyze the Problem

Your first step is to make sure you're dealing with the right problem. Identifying the problem correctly is key. As an example, suppose a reporter is not covering her beat effectively. When you talk about it with her, she asks you for another beat. Your problem appears to be one of assigning her to a new beat and finding her replacement, or leaving her where she is. If you accept this as the problem, without further investigation, you may end up dealing with the wrong issue, and along the way, creating a new problem. Instead, a number of issues could underlie the reporter's request:

- She may not see a future for her byline if she remains in her current beat.
- She may not be getting cooperation from colleagues.
- She may simply dislike the beat.
- She may be pursuing the wrong stories, which may be why she fails to get into print or on the air regularly.
- The beat is too difficult for her.
- She may be unhappy with her editor.
- She may really want to transfer to a different area of the organization.
- She may need help in developing her skills.

Let's look at how you can make sure that you deal with the problem itself rather than the symptoms of the problem as you conduct your analysis. Using the reporter's request for another beat as an example, you would start by investigating the reasons for the request. What could cause this reporter to want to switch beats? Is she bored? Or simply doing a poor job? If either is true, perhaps you've also noticed a poor attitude. That might be caused by a lack of motivation. Or perhaps the cause of a problem is poor team work in this reporter's section. Take a look at the performance of others in the same section:

- Has there been a pattern of high turnover?
- Are some of the reporters doing an outstanding job, while others are listless or doing just enough to get by?
- Is the work being done by other reporters satisfactory?
- If the work is not satisfactory, were those reporters doing a better job six months ago, for example?
- Was the reporter who wants to change her beat doing a better job six months ago?

After you've answered questions such as these you'll be more confident that you're dealing with the right problem rather than a symptom of it.

Research the Problem

You may be tempted to skip this second step because you've already analyzed the problem. But your analysis could delude you into thinking that because you have *some* information about the problem, you're ready to solve it. A quick-fix solution might create more problems than it solves. That's why further research is so important. Research requires you to focus on specifics and helps you be sure the same problem has not happened in the past.

In the example of the reporter requesting a new beat, you would review your department's records. You'd try to find out if previous editors had the same problem with the same reporter or with the same beat. You might look through personnel files of reporters who have worked in your newsroom for the past three years. Has one person been a long-term employee while others have not lasted very long? That long-term reporter might have a penchant for wielding power, making life difficult for colleagues, or snapping up the best stories. The reporter who wants to change her beat may not be getting opportunities because of that long-term reporter.

This is the kind of information that can help you make sure you are dealing with the right problem. Research doesn't necessarily provide a solution to the problem, but it does help you to examine it in a different way.

During this stage, it is important to focus on specifics. Use the five Ws of writing as a guide: *Who* did it, *what* did they do, *where, when,* and *why.* This is where your journalistic training can help you deal with a problem. Find out how long this problem has been going on. For example, you may learn from personnel that the reporter who wants to change her beat is often late to work. But even that information, by itself, is not enough. You want to know how many times, in what period, and her explanations.

If you talk to others about the reporter, try to get more than a general response. Only specific data will help you resolve a specific problem. Let's say you ask her immediate editor about her performance. "She turns in stories late" doesn't tell you much. What does "late" mean? A more specific response might reveal the reporter always struggles to do one more interview right at deadline or spends too much time writing the lead. Or "turns in stories late" could mean simply that she is disorganized and puts off work until deadline.

Get as much information as you reasonably can but set a time limit. Avoid looking only for information that will support a position or a decision you have already chosen rather than searching for information that will help solve the problem.

Find the Cause

At this point you're ready to examine the information you've gathered and reflect on possible causes of the problem. Ferreting out the cause is not always an easy task. The most apparent cause may not be the true one.

For example, if a reporter is apparently having trouble getting along with others, the cause may not necessarily be related to personality. A calculating reporter may be keeping important information to himself and may have adopted an aggressive attitude to keep colleagues at bay. Or the reporter who asked for a transfer to another beat may feel the stories she is writing are not as important as those written by others. Colleagues may complain that she doesn't cooperate, when in reality she may be trying to make her own stories seem more important by telling others that she has too much work to cooperate with them.

If the same problem has come up in the past, why is the problem resurfacing now? Has another editor, in solving a problem, created a new situation that generated the current difficulty? Perhaps the reporter's previous editor simply ignored this problem, feeling that a solution would be too expensive or complicated to implement. Or maybe the previous editor's solution solved only part of the problem. Perhaps the previous editor's solution was excellent, but was never fully implemented. Or perhaps it did resolve the problem, but only temporarily, because a new element has now altered conditions.

Consider the Alternatives

Before you decide on a specific solution, consider every alternative. Remember, you want the best solution, not the first one that comes to mind. At this stage brainstorm as many solutions as you can. Write the alternatives down.

If you take your time considering alternatives you will be confident that you have considered all the options and can present your reasons for rejecting each. This is especially useful if a superior doesn't like the solution you selected. It will be much easier for you to defend your final decision if you can present the alternative courses of action you considered and your reasons for rejecting each one.

Choose the Solution

You switch now from analysis of the problem to the decision-making process. As you evaluate your solution, keep these three considerations in mind.

1. Is your solution realistic? Considering the people involved, the conditions, your budget, and other factors relevant to this specific case, will this solution really work? If you anticipate resistance, what can you do to encourage acceptance? Carrying out a solution should not be difficult, although editors can sometimes make it so by not anticipating problems.

2. Will your solution be accepted? Will this reporter, and her colleagues, accept your solution? Are there factors you have not considered that would make acceptance difficult or impossible?[1] Will it fit their individual personalities or routines? Will it fit with the way they work with each other? Or, if this is a problem that involves newsroom procedures or policies, will those involved willingly accept the new policy or be able to adapt to it?
3. Is your solution appropriate? Will this solution solve the problem in these circumstances at this time? Can you defend this solution if it is challenged? Will it be accepted by management? Will you be able to defend it as the only viable solution?

Implementing the Solution

When you have selected what you feel is the suitable solution, write it down along with your reasons. This is especially important in case you need to defend your decision.[2] Use a form like the one shown in Figure 7.1 to document your decision.

Communicating the Decision

Most of your work now involves communicating your decision to those involved. Make sure you don't miss anyone. List those who will be involved

Figure 7.1 The Problem, Solution, and Reasons

The Problem
_____
_____

The Solution
_____
_____

The Reasons
_____
_____

Figure 7.2 Decision Implementation Checklist

Who should be informed about this decision? (Examples: Your superior, management, other newsroom staff, personnel in other departments, photography, the IT department) _____

Who will be affected? _____

Will anyone be moved to another location? _____ Who? _____

Where will the person or persons be moved to? _____

Will they have new or different job responsibilities? _____

What are the new responsibilities? _____

Who will oppose this solution? _____

Which reporters will you ask initially to accept this solution? _____

What risks are involved? _____

Who is likely to misunderstand what you are attempting to do? _____

Does your superior agree with this solution? ❏ Yes ❏ No

Will your superior support you if there is opposition to your idea? ❏ Yes ❏ No

---

and try to determine how they will react. A sample checklist appears in Figure 7.2.

Deciding to Take No Action

You may discover that none of the solutions you have come up with will resolve the problem or that they have been tried before and have failed to resolve the issue. Perhaps you have simply run out of time. Maybe none of the alternatives that are available are acceptable to the parties involved or to management. In such cases you still have one option left: to do nothing at all. There may be times when you'll want to consider this option, since some problems resolve themselves.

For example, imagine a major story that a team is working on under intense pressure to beat the competition. As a journalist you have probably experienced such a situation. Tempers flare, sometimes triggered by mistakes resulting from the pressure or from someone taking too long to deliver copy or missing facts. Reporters may bark at each other, criticize each other, even yell at each other. Once the crisis atmosphere dies down and things return to normal, problems caused by too many people working under too much pressure will disappear.

However, there's a down side to the no-action solution. That's the danger in taking the approach that every problem will resolve itself eventually. Many editors have developed serious stress problems waiting for problems to disappear.

You can't always wait for the problem to resolve itself, but you can determine whether this problem has a history of repeating itself. For example, some reporters will always complain if they don't get their way. In other words, know your people well enough to take steps to avoid the problem in the first place. For example, if you expect opposition from someone, make sure that person cooperates early in the execution of the decision, since getting that person to buy in later will be much more difficult.

Follow-Up

After you set the solution in motion, you'll need to monitor it to make sure everything is going according to your expectations. An occasional spot check will tell you if the plan is running on course.

During this follow-up phase, try not to become so enamored of your solution that you fail to detect when it is not working. Ask yourself whether the problem really is solved or just went away for a while and may resurface. If the problem persists, you may need to ask for help from a superior.

Involving Reporters in Problem Solving

Bringing reporters into the process is integral in problem analysis and decision making. Reporters represent much more to their organizations than simply a means to an end. They can impact decisions at the highest level and even corporate policy. As media organizations grow globally, reporters often acquire as much knowledge about the newspaper or station, and what it takes to improve the quality of the news being produced, as those who supervise them.

What's more, reporters are increasingly involved in the technical side of producing news products. Their intimate knowledge of the production process provides you, as their supervisor, with a superb opportunity to work with them in solving problems. That opportunity can be hampered, however, if you feel that reporters will make poor, uninformed, or irrelevant suggestions because they don't understand how to run a newsroom. When problems surface this attitude often prevents editors from asking for input from those who report to them.

Often this is a result of a misunderstanding of the process. Problem analysis is an effort to ferret out a cause as well as a solution, as we have seen. When you analyze a problem, you are looking for a circumstance, or set of circumstances, that created the present condition. Because few problems can be resolved if their cause is not detected and understood, you might reach an inaccurate conclusion if you attempt to resolve a problem without input from those involved.

You have been brought into the situation because the person with the problem was unable to resolve it alone. This is an excellent opportunity, if time permits, to train this reporter in the steps involved in problem solving. Encouraging reporters to participate in problem solving qualifies you as an enlightened editor in the new workplace of the twenty-first century. Your reporters will be better prepared to manage problems themselves in the future and thus help you manage your newsroom as well.

When a reporter helps solve a problem, motivation ratchets up dramatically: The reporter owns the solution, with consequent enthusiastic commitment. Pride in ownership of the solution helps ensure that this problem, in any case, is less likely to resurface.

Use the problem-solving worksheet in Figure 7.3 every time you need to analyze, research, and develop alternatives to problems.

Sometimes the problems reporters bring to you will be concerns about the workplace. How you deal with those concerns can affect morale in your newsroom. In the next chapter we look at techniques for dealing with complaints about the workplace brought to you, as well as requirements to protect whistleblowers.

Notes

1. In one case, an editor asked several reporters to work extra hours on a special section to meet a deadline. One of the reporters was unable to work those hours because she had to pick up her child at a certain time from day care. The editor didn't know about this and considered the reporter's refusal to work extra hours as insubordination. In this case, the solution to the problem was realistic but it was not acceptable.

2. In our litigious society, some decisions may be challenged in court, so it just makes sense to document your decisions and the reasons for them.

Figure 7.3 Problem-Solving Worksheet

Phase One

As you investigate, write down an accurate description of the problem and work out a profile of any significant events that may have contributed to it. Make sure the description is *clear*. Describe the event in language that others, who may review your report later, can easily understand. Make sure it is *concise*. An essay is unnecessary when several sentences may be all you need to describe the problem accurately. Use only enough words to make your description clear.

_____

_____

_____

_____

_____

_____

_____

Phase Two

1. What kind of problem are you dealing with?
   - ❏ Procedure
   - ❏ Training
   - ❏ Policy
   - ❏ Technology
   - ❏ Other _____

2. What is your analysis of the problem?

   _____

   _____

3. Research

   Is this a new or a recurring problem?   ❏ New   ❏ Recurring

   Answer the five specifics:

   Who _____

   What _____

   Where _____

When _____

Why _____

4. What is the cause of the problem? _____
5. What is the history of the problem? _____
6. Has the problem happened before? ❏ Yes ❏ No

   What happened previously? _____
   _____

7. What are the alternative solutions?

   a. _____
   b. _____
   c. _____

8. Develop choices to solve the problem.

   Choice One _____
   Choice Two _____
   Choice Three _____
   Choice Four _____

9. Evaluate your choices against the following criteria:

   • Is the solution you have selected realistic?
   • Is the solution you have selected workable?
   • Can you defend this solution if it is challenged?

   Alternative Choice One _____
   Alternative Choice Two _____
   Alternative Choice Three _____
   Alternative Choice Four _____

10. Who should be informed about this decision? _____
    Who will be affected? _____
    Will anyone be moved? Who? _____
    Where will the person or persons be moved to? _____
    What will be their new job responsibilities? _____
    _____

(continued)

(continued)

  Who will oppose this solution? _____

  Which reporters will you ask initially to accept this solution?

  _____

  What risks are involved? _____

  Who is likely to misunderstand what you are attempting to do? _____

  Does your superior agree with this solution? ❑ Yes ❑ No

  Will your superior support you? ❑ Yes ❑ No

11. What is the best solution to this problem?

  _____

  _____

  _____

  Reasons:

  _____

  _____

  _____

12. Prepare to implement the solution.
13. Implement the solution.
14. Monitor execution of the solution.

  Dates for follow-up: _____

15. Was the solution successful? ❑ Yes ❑ No Date _____

  Explanation _____

Phase Three

Lessons learned from this problem-solving exercise:

_____

_____

_____

8 Handling Reporter Concerns

After you finish this chapter, you will be able to:
- Analyze criticism, complaints, and concerns
- Handle employee concerns skillfully and competently
- Investigate thoroughly to comply with laws and regulations
- Comply with whistleblower laws that protect the rights of concerned reporters

Introduction

Even when you think you're doing everything right, and the newsroom is humming with happy people, there will be criticism of your management style. You won't be aware of most of the grumbling and probably wouldn't want to hear it anyway. Perhaps it's the nature of journalists to complain. Most reporters, producers, photographers, and broadcast news personnel are justifiably proud of their publication or station and believe they are better than their competition. At the same time, they find it easy to complain about their workplace. Some complaints may come from perennial whiners. Other complainers may just have a need to be heard. Some may be dissatisfied with conditions that their former editor never addressed. And some may have serious, legitimate concerns.

If you are a new editor, just promoted to your position, you may feel uncomfortable supervising reporters who were once your colleagues. You have an advantage, however: You're familiar with many of the problems as well as the strengths of your department. If you are a seasoned editor, but new to your organization, you may have inherited problems. Either way, your job is, in part, to solve them.

Reporters will watch how you handle your job. They may compare you with the former editor at first, scrutinize your management style, and make hasty conclusions. No matter how well you do, some will find fault. On the other hand, most reporters will accept you as editor and get on with the job.

It is important to establish a climate of openness and immediate attention to concerns at the outset. You want to know about discontent. You want the reporters to know that they can trust you to investigate thoroughly and take decisive action. The last thing you want is to hear about a problem from an attorney—or on the evening news.

Handling Reporters' Concerns

As a new editor, you will learn soon after you assume command that reporter concerns fall into four general categories: the system, the workplace, personal treatment, or behavior of others in the department.

Reporters can take up chunks of time from your busy schedule if you grant them adequate attention when they have a concern. Failure to do so, every editor soon learns, can often result in a larger chunk of valuable time lost later in damage control. When a reporter comes to you with a concern, deal with it as soon as you can. Often, an incident snowballs to a crisis because it was not dealt with promptly. On the other hand, when you take time to discuss the concern, you send a message that you respect the people who report to you and will do whatever is necessary to ensure a safe and respectful workplace environment.

Attention and respect are essential when you listen to a reporter's concerns. Not all concerns can be resolved; not all of them are even valid. The secret to fairness is to make the reporter feel confident that, at the time you deal with a concern, the reporter and the issue are receiving serious consideration and will receive a serious response, whether or not the solution meets the reporter's expectations.

Acknowledge every employee concern. Ideally, you will learn about a concern when the reporter comes to you—a "walk-in interview." However, your first indication of a problem might come from an angry outburst in an editorial meeting, for example, or in the newsroom. Although it is better to handle reporter concerns privately, you may have to deal with a problem immediately and publicly. Your safest policy is to urge the reporter to meet you later to discuss the problem confidentially. Let the reporter decide. If the reporter wants to deal with the concern at once, and in public, let him or her continue.

In many cases, the reporter may seem exasperated, even angry. But anger often conceals deeper feelings. You may have to investigate beyond the angry outburst to discover the true problem. Typically an angry reporter is:

- Indignant over a violation of the law
- Concerned about environmental problems in the workplace
- Frustrated with the system
- Humiliated by a person or an incident
- Upset over discrimination, whether real or imagined

Discuss concerns promptly. Once you've been made aware of the concern, discuss it promptly. The reporter has a right to this. Moreover, the reporter may have already decided on a deadline for resolution of the problem that you are unaware of.

Professional employee concern. Investigators call this an unknown deadline. For example, the reporter may have attempted to resolve the issue on his or her own, been ignored, and come to you as a last resort. In some instances, if you don't move quickly, the reporter may have an attorney's telephone number ready. Maintain a serious and businesslike demeanor.

Select a suitable place to meet. In your initial conversation with the reporter, stick to the facts. Don't voice any conclusions. Meet in your office so you can control distractions. If the person voicing the concern has called you on the phone, however, deal with it immediately; don't wait to set up an interview. Of course, if the person you're talking to is in a different location, another city for example, a phone interview is unavoidable.

Project a positive attitude during the interview. Be aware of your body language. Don't roll your eyes, tap your fingers, or appear impatient. Even if this reporter is a chronic complainer, this may be the one time he or she is right.

Get directly to the point. Make the reporter feel comfortable immediately. Ask the reporter to explain the purpose of this interview as soon as possible. Then allow the reporter to describe the concern in detail. As you listen, mentally note any clarifying questions you may have.

Let the reporter finish without interruption. Then try to sum up the concern with a statement that begins with a direct reference to the emotion: "You seem indignant because . . ." and summarize the concern. For example, you might say "You're annoyed because you've asked this person to stop making offensive gestures and it hasn't stopped." Or, "You're seriously concerned that the drinking water may be toxic and you want something done about it."

If you believe the reporter's perception of the situation is unrealistic, do not attempt to point this out. Rather, express empathy; what a concerned employee wants most of all is to be heard. "I'm sorry you feel that way," you might say. "I'll investigate your concern to gather all the information I can."

If you are the person the reporter is angry with, address the issue immediately. Begin with, "I'm sorry you feel like that. I'd like to explain my point of view so you can understand."

Many editors ask whether a reporter's motivation for blowing the whistle should be a consideration. The answer is no. Just deal with the issue being reported. Ignore the reporter's motivation for complaining since there may well be a hidden agenda. For example, a reporter may meet with you to blow the whistle on an ex-lover in retaliation for being jilted. That motivation (lover's quarrel) should have no bearing on your investigation. Handle the issue, not the hidden agenda.

Question diligently. Be careful not to ask close-ended questions. Close-ended questions evoke a yes or no response. Open-ended questions generate more information. Use your interviewing skills when discussing reporter concerns.

When dealing with a reporter's concern, start with general questions, then get into specifics. Avoid leading questions, which can prompt the reporter to respond with a specific answer. If the reporter doesn't know the answer, you might get your own question back as an answer. If you ask too many leading questions, the reporter might decide to tell you what you want to hear.

In other words, don't provide the answer in the question: "You have a gray car, don't you?" Finally, keep your questions simple. Don't ask for two or three answers in one question.

Agree on the issue. Once you have the facts, make sure that the reporter and you agree on the issue. If you don't agree on a clear understanding of the issue to be resolved, the reporter may walk away from your meeting with a different idea of what was discussed, fail to see it resolved, and later feel ignored.

Before ending the conversation, summarize the information you have received. Give the reporter a chance to review your understanding of the problem and make changes. "Correct me if I'm wrong," you might say, or "Did I miss anything?" There are several reasons why this is important:

- You'll verify the information you have received and make sure that the reporter agrees with your understanding of the issue being reported.
- You'll be able to determine whether there are multiple issues. If so, write them all down.
- You'll provide the reporter with a chance to furnish additional information. Given the opportunity, whistleblowers invariably remember

additional information during a summation. This information can help you in your investigation.
- You'll prevent the reporter from later changing or denying some aspect of what was said.

Often, concerned reporters will also suggest a solution for a matter they report. If the solution is unrealistic or impossible to carry out, ask for another idea. Say you will consider the suggestions, but make no commitment. Finally, thank the reporter for taking the time to come to you to discuss the concern and tell the individual your next step.

Investigation

Here are four common mistakes many editors make when investigating complaints.

1. Failure to prepare adequately. This is the most frequent cause of extra work in investigations.
2. Failure to adopt a positive mental attitude. This can be an especially serious drawback if you are dealing with politically sensitive or highly complex issues.
3. Failure to specify a goal for the investigation with the whistleblower. Often, editors will complicate a simple issue. Try to make the issue as simple as possible. On the other hand, don't attempt to oversimplify.
4. Failure to take notes. If taking notes is not practical, try to tape record all interviews. Be sure to ask for permission to record before you begin. To make certain that the permission is chronicled, your first question can be, "I am taping this conversation with the permission of (name the reporter)."

You will need to document your investigation. Your first document should be your record of the reporter's concern. Write a complete record and offer the reporter an opportunity to sign it, although this should not be a requirement. Use a form similar to the one provided in Figure 8.1.

Use a folder for your file with notes in the left pocket and documents in the right pocket. If you're investigating in the newsroom, carry your file with you along with a pad for notes. Never put notes about the investigation in your day planner: If the issue should go to court, your entire diary can be subpoenaed, and there may be items in your planner you don't want revealed.

Document thoroughly because if the concern is serious, you don't take prompt action, or the reporter is not satisfied, the problem could end up in

Figure 8.1 Reporter Concern Interview Form

Date _____ Supervising Editor _____

Reporter _____

Summary of Concern

_____
_____
_____
_____
_____
_____
_____
_____
_____
_____
_____
_____

Signature _____ Date _____

court. "Juries tend to believe people over companies and documents over testimony," says Dennis Hamilton, an Illinois consultant who worked for 17 years as an investigator and now conducts training on principles of investigation.

Here's a list of the kinds of documents you will want to collect:

- Statements of company policies and procedures
- Copies of relevant regulations and laws
- Computer logs
- Evidence of complaints or similar incidents

Your documents should be timely, thorough, organized, and neat. They should have a professional appearance because documents can be challenged if there are mistakes or alterations in them, or if they are incomplete. One way you can keep track of your investigation is to use a form such as the one in Figure 8.2.

Figure 8.2 Complaint Investigation

Investigation

Date of Incident _____ Time of Incident _____

Individuals Involved (if applicable)
_____
_____

Date of Interview _____ Time/date of meeting _____

Summary of interviews by (name):
_____
_____
_____
_____
_____
_____

Date of Interview _____ Time/date of meeting _____

Summary of interviews by (name):
_____
_____
_____
_____
_____
_____

Date of Interview _____ Time/date of meeting _____

List of documents reviewed and summary of conclusions:
_____
_____
_____
_____
_____
_____

Violence in the Workplace

Violence in the workplace is a growing concern. Violence can come from outside the newsroom, but it can also erupt inside. Officials who work in this field have not yet developed a profile of a person who may be likely to carry out a violent act. Until a solution to workplace violence is found, your best defense is to develop a workplace violence prevention program, similar to your reporter concern program. Since reporters' stories can sometimes provoke violent reactions, your organization may already have security measures in place. Inside the newsroom, disgruntled, disappointed, or emotional reporters, those who might have an addiction problem, and persons who are fascinated with violence or small arms may become violent.

A circuit court judge suggests one method to cope with violence in the workplace is to provide conflict resolution training. Ask your human resources department to design such a workshop for everyone who reports to you.

Ten Guidelines for Handling Reporter Concerns

Follow these ten guidelines when you receive a complaint from a reporter.

1. When dealing with emotional situations
   a. Acknowledge the emotion.
   b. Investigate the issue.
   c. Resolve the issue.
   d. Determine whether the reporter feels differently after the issue is resolved.
2. Give every serious complaint serious consideration. Reporters must feel confident you will investigate and take action when warranted. Keep in mind that this person feels that you are the person to turn to for resolution of this complaint, even if you are the person the reporter is angry with.
3. Eliminate distractions. Don't pick up the phone, or make a call, or allow another person to interrupt during the initial interview.
4. Provide positive feedback. Let the reporter know you are paying attention and making an effort to listen and understand.
5. Do not argue with the reporter even if the complaint is directed at you and you feel it is unfair. Listen to the reporter. Promise to review your actions. You are not admitting guilt; you are only stating you will examine your own behavior to see whether the complaint has merit. You can examine the complaint after the reporter leaves.

6. Ask questions to narrow the complaint. Try to determine whether the problem has been going on for some time or is new. Ask for specifics: names, dates, times, and examples. Deal only with facts.
7. Never ask the reporter to explain another's behavior. "Why on earth would so-and-so do something like that?" is a question that seldom has an answer.
8. Summarize the complaint as accurately as possible in a written statement. When you finish, read your summary back to the reporter and incorporate changes until you have a statement the reporter can agree to. Suggest the reporter sign it.
9. Ask the reporter to suggest a solution. Say you will consider it. Avoid making hasty decisions when others are involved until all parties have had a chance to present their positions. You might solve one complaint while creating a new one.
10. End the meeting with an affirmative statement. "I appreciate your coming to me about this and your confidence in me." This will help to assure that the reporter will feel free to come to you again with future problems.

Foster an Employee Concern Environment

Reporters who are concerned about unacceptable conduct or conditions in your department may hesitate to come forward. They may fear retaliation from colleagues—whistleblowers are not always treated fairly—or they may think their concern will be ignored or that management doesn't want to hear about problems. So it's important to foster a climate that encourages reporting incidents, especially those that could be a violation of federal or state laws. One way to do this is to set up an employee concern program in your department. Assure reporters that they can meet with you to express concerns at any time. As part of this program, make sure reporters know that they are protected when they come forward: Whistleblowers are protected under federal law and retaliation is prohibited.[1]

Employee concerns are just one illustration of how intensely and seriously journalists take their job. This zeal can sometimes erupt in emotional outbursts. Whether or not you are comfortable dealing with emotional flare-ups, your staff will look to you to handle them. In the next chapter you will look at techniques for handling emotional displays in your newsroom.

Note

1. See a sampling of whisleblower laws in the Appendix.

9 Dealing with Emotions

After you finish this chapter, you will be able to:
- Understand four common causes of emotional outbursts in the newsroom
- Distinguish between work-related and personal emotional issues
- Know when to remain silent and when to speak
- Deal with an emotional outburst effectively

Introduction

Unless you are a keen observer of human nature who can discern tension building among reporters, emotional displays will usually surprise you. Emotional eruptions generally demand your complete and immediate attention. Your success in dealing with emotional issues may well depend, therefore, on your skill at rapid response.

As a journalist, you wrote about the emotional displays of people in the news, while you remained objective and removed from those displays. As a journalist, no one expected you to step in and calm down or comfort someone who was caught up in the moment. Now that you are an editor, you can no longer remain aloof. When there is an emotional outburst in your newsroom you are expected to step in and do something. Many editors may feel their skills in this area are inadequate. However, unless there is some specialist in your organization trained to successfully manage emotional outbursts, your team will look to you for leadership in this area.

Consistently tense work in the close confines of a newsroom is enough to create pressure among even the most laid-back reporters. Add to that the number-one characteristic of journalism—inflexible deadlines—and you have the ingredients for a cauldron of newsroom emotions. Emotional problems cannot be ignored, avoided, or dismissed. Moreover, if they are not resolved, they can fester and grow into resentments, which ultimately cause serious problems.

Causes of Emotional Outbursts

While emotional outbursts can be triggered by a variety of causes, we'll confine this review to four of the most common causes of emotional outbursts in a newsroom: ambition, envy, jealousy, and low self-esteem.

Ambition

Although fairly easy to recognize, ambition can be deceptively covert. You already know what ambition feels like: To become a supervisor, you needed ambition yourself. Ambition is essential in an assertive reporter. It becomes dangerous, however, when it tramples on the rights of others.

Dealing with reporters' ambitions successfully can be tricky. You want to contain uncontrolled ambition when others are hurt, yet you want to avoid stifling it in promising reporters. Ambition usually is a positive force that will contribute to a better news report.

Deal with ambition by channeling it productively into work that is challenging and gratifying. Ambition lusts for recognition; more work and faster promotion often satisfies that need. But keep a defensive eye on ambitious people. They will take over if you let them.

Envy

Envy is far more difficult to deal with than ambition. Envy is a longing to have something that someone else has, from a nicer car or home to a better beat or a fancier desk. You may not recognize envy since people try to keep it hidden. Envy can be consuming and destructive; it can eat away at less-talented writers.

Deal with envy by providing skills training. A feeling of competence often neutralizes envy.

Jealousy

Jealousy can be triggered when people feel discriminated against or treated as inferior to others. Resentments frequently build on a foundation of jealousy. It can be successfully disguised: Most people don't like to admit they are jealous of others.

As editor, you might trigger jealousy quite unintentionally if you spend too much time with reporters you consider friends, or favor them consistently with choice stories or soft editing.

Deal with jealousy by examining your own role in creating it if you suspect reporters have made up their minds that you are playing favorites. Make sure everyone gets equal treatment in the newsroom. Keep reporters intensely busy and they will spend more time worrying about how they deal with their stories than worrying about how you or others treat them.

Low Self-Esteem

Lack of confidence can lead to blow-ups. People who lack confidence in their own abilities look for ways to compensate. They may conjure up imagined offenses and turn them into rumors. What they're doing is building themselves up by tearing others down—you or coworkers. The reporter may constantly criticize the work of others, pointing out mistakes, weaknesses, or oversights. This can trigger quarrelsome relationships, even divisiveness. These people are seldom aware that their divisive behavior affects the respect others have for them in the newsroom.

Dealing with low self-esteem is especially difficult since these people often sabotage themselves. They sometimes express their low opinion of themselves with manifestations of superiority. They may consider themselves unworthy of assistance and reject it or argue that your help won't ease their problem, which they may deny or even refuse to recognize. Offering people training in skills they feel they lack can relieve low self-esteem, but in most cases the person who suffers from low self-esteem is the person who has to correct it.

Your Comfort Level in Emotional Situations

Do you find tearful situations unpleasant? Are you uncomfortable when others behave emotionally? Were you brought up to believe that people are not supposed to show their emotions at work, or that weeping is a sign of weakness? If so, you need to shed such beliefs: Emotional expression is an essential part of the human makeup, including in the workplace.

If you are uncomfortable in an emotional situation, you may withdraw or even avoid it, consciously or subconsciously. One method people use to cope with emotion is literally to turn their backs and leave. Another method is to attempt to make the person exhibiting the emotion stop. Demanding that a person stop crying, for example, assumes that the tears are the cause, rather than the symptom. But even when the crying stops, the unhappiness, frustration, anger, or other emotions may remain.

As a supervisor, you can't simply walk away from an emotional outburst. It is your responsibility to take steps to resolve emotional situations. If you simply insist a person stop, the underlying cause will remain. Moreover, if you halt an emotional scene prematurely, you prevent it from exhausting itself. This can be a mistake.

You need to learn how to bring the situation back to a normal level and then proceed to get help from the appropriate sources.

Managing an Emotional Outburst

When to Keep Silent and When to Speak

When a reporter bursts into tears or rage, the best initial reaction is to remain silent and allow the emotional outburst to drain. Many emotional eruptions in the workplace are a consequence of frustration that has been building up over time. Anger, which almost always covers up another deeper emotion, often reflects frustration. Don't be confused by the event that triggers the outburst if it seems trivial: It may be the last in a series of events, the final straw.

If you tell the reporter, "Stop crying so we can talk about this calmly," you might arrest the reporter's emotional outburst too soon. The reporter needs the release and needs it now. If it is halted, it may simply manifest itself later, and you may not be the person the reporter calls on in the future for help. The reporter needs to see you now as a person who can be counted on to understand.

Figure 9.1 lists statements that you might make in attempting to deal with a reporter in an emotional outburst. Check those you think would help.

Although a reporter may be angry when venting emotions, avoid getting caught up in that anger. The person may be unreasonable, shout, or use unacceptable language. The temptation to shout is irresistible sometimes. But shouting may cause you to lose your own temper.

Avoid arguing with someone who is angry. Reporters who are agitated can say unpleasant things about the company or about your leadership, which you may feel compelled to answer. Defending yourself immediately against such charges could lead to a heated exchange. Editors who lose their tempers lose control.

Figure 9.1 Emotional Statements

☐ 1. "I wouldn't handle it that way if I were you."

☐ 2. "I will try to understand what you are going through."

☐ 3. "That's such a minor problem; I don't see why you're so upset over it."

☐ 4. "That has happened to me, and I didn't cry over it."

☐ 5. "I see how important this is to you."

☐ 6. "Get a grip on yourself! You'll never solve problems by losing your temper or crying about them."

☐ 7. "If I were you I wouldn't be envious of that person over such a small thing."

☐ 8. "I want to try to empathize with what you are feeling."

Statements 2, 5, and 8 are good choices and will be helpful. When people are in an emotional state, they expect sympathy.

Statements 1, 3, 4, 6, and 7 are aggressive or judgmental.

In statements 1, 3, and 7 the editor is passing judgment on the emotional response. It is important not to express judgment on the appropriateness of the emotional reaction of the reporter while it is being manifested.

Statements 4 and 6 are aggressive. They would cause the emotional person to sense criticism or censure and become defensive. This only locks out any receptiveness to solving the issue.

Investigate the Cause

After you have endured the tempest, you need to deal with the emotion that triggered it. Give the reporter time to vent, unless a dangerous element is present (for example, a weapon). The source of an emotional eruption is not always easy to distinguish during a flare-up. The underlying cause of the problem may be a recent issue or lie in the distant past. It may turn out to be work-related, which will make your task easier, or entirely personal. After the outburst subsides, you can initiate the fact-finding phase.

Help the reporter focus on the problem rather than the emotion. As you begin to deal with the situation calmly, permit the reporter to describe his or her frustration, even if it includes accusations. This may well be all the reporter needs to understand that his or her problems may not have an immediate solution.

Sometimes a reporter will be embarrassed and lapse into silence after an initial outburst. The reporter may not want to add to his or her discomfort by continuing, especially if the display took place in front of coworkers. Because it is important that the reporter talk about the issue so that you can resolve the problem, suggest that both of you go to a more private place, such as your office, an empty hall, the lunchroom, or an office not being used. Walk there quickly with the reporter. People who have been upset in front of coworkers and are feeling embarrassed will welcome the suggestion to escape.

Focus on the Underlying Problem

Asking a person, "Why are you crying?" is unproductive. An emotional person needs to detach and contribute information to an objective assessment of the underlying cause. An emotional outburst often masks the true problem: People in the throes of anger or tears may be describing how they feel rather than what is causing it.

For example, a reporter comes to you and bursts out, "I've been assigned to do obituaries three days in a row for the last four weeks. Every time it's Shirley's turn to write obits I have to take them." When the reporter calms down, she may reveal the true cause of her discomfort: "No one makes Shirley write obits because she's the boss's favorite."

Notice how the reporter confused her frustration over writing obituaries too frequently with jealousy because of presumed (or real) favoritism toward another reporter. Such a confused interpretation is not unusual. People may give you several versions of the cause during the outburst.

Or they may say things that are inconsistent. For example, the school beat reporter has been turning in uninspired copy. When you bring this to her attention, she bursts into tears. She complains that her beat generates routine stories while others cover stories that are more glamorous. "No one reads what I write," she says. Your best response to an emotional reaction such as this is to empathize: "I understand that you are upset." After the reporter calms down, you can ask, "Why do you think you are losing readers?" Asking open-ended questions encourages the reporter to reveal the underlying cause of the emotional outburst. The reporter answers, "Everyone is interested in high tech these days. There's not much interest in school news. You're going to stop running my stories eventually and I could lose my job." "What makes you think that would happen?"

you ask. She reveals that her sister was laid off recently and her worry about her sister's future has caused her to be concerned about her own. Without a job, she can't help her sister.

Notice that initially, the reporter complained about the beat. As she continued, she talked about another issue—layoffs. That led to discussion of the real problem, her sister's predicament. You ask for more information about her sister.

"My sister has two children—she may have to move in with me. I can't afford the extra expense." The true concern, then, is fear of losing something she has, her job, at a time when she is needed. Worried, she searches for a real or imagined threat to that job and decides her stories are uninteresting. She looks for a scapegoat and seizes on the trendy stories making the front page. She assumes, erroneously, that they will make the work she does irrelevant.

By listening and encouraging the reporter to talk through the emotion, you can find the true cause of the problem.

Encourage the Reporter to Suggest a Solution

Before you try to solve the problem yourself, ask the reporter for suggestions. "What ideas do you have to deal with this?" you might ask. Because they are so personal, solutions to emotional concerns ought to come from the reporter when possible. Ask the reporter to help you develop a solution. Frequently, the reporter will already have one.

Before you adopt the solution, take your time to examine its consequences. If the reporter's proposed solution seems acceptable, you might adopt it. If the suggestion isn't viable, discuss alternatives. In either case, the reporter will be satisfied you have listened and have been understanding.

You have now moved from an emotional situation to a reasoned discussion and a possible solution.

Sometimes, however, problems are more behavioral than emotional and can cause far more serious consequences for the individual. Behavioral problems take you into a new area: discipline. In the next chapter we review techniques to deal with unsatisfactory behavior.

10 Counseling to Change Unsatisfactory Behavior

After you finish this chapter, you will be able to:
- Counsel a reporter to help change unsatisfactory behavior
- Plan and carry out a meeting to change unsatisfactory behavior
- Understand four progressive actions to change behavior
- Distinguish between counseling, warning, discipline, and punishment

Introduction

As a leader who gets work done through others, you may consider yourself successful when all those who report to you carry out their responsibilities with little supervision. Sometimes, however, unsatisfactory behavior interferes with the smooth functioning of your newsroom and you will have to intervene to correct it. That means counseling, warnings, or discipline, all of which are unpleasant but effective when carried out correctly.

Leadership by example would be enough in an ideal newsroom, but no newsroom is ideal. Reporters break rules, arrive late, miss deadlines, leave their workspace untidy, argue with colleagues, wisecrack to superiors or to people they deal with, abuse electronic and other equipment, turn in poor or unacceptable work, or fail to report problems. Positive example doesn't always work in such cases.

Your first choice should always be to help the reporter change the behavior. Your company has made a considerable investment in this person. Besides that, you chose this reporter because of his or her ability and promise. Counseling often is all that is needed for a reporter to change unsatisfactory workplace habits. When necessary, discipline gets the attention of a worthwhile reporter and helps raise his or her performance to the expected standard.

Encouraging Positive Behavior

Reporters are expected to perform to a previously determined standard. Generally, the reporter agrees to abide by the organization's standards when he or she accepts the job, and receives and reads the employee manual. But from time to time reporters may need to be informed or reminded of the standard and encouraged to meet it. There are five ways you can do this, as outlined in Table 10.1.

Table 10.1 Five Ways to Encourage Positive Behavior

OPTION	
Practice: Leadership by establishing a model of the desired behavior.	*Practice stimulates change by example.* As a leader you meet or exceed standards on a daily basis. Reporters observe your example and emulate you. Your own behavior reminds reporters that they have agreed to perform to a standard. This should be enough to discourage unsatisfactory behavior in most reporters who have a positive attitude.
Prompt: Reminder of a standard of performance that all agreed to.	*Prompting stimulates change by reminder.* You remind all reporters during a staff meeting, for example, of the department's standards, emphasizing those that are not being observed. This indirect method doesn't single out any individual.
Counsel: Direct intervention to change the poor workplace habit.	*Counseling stimulates change by advice or by admonition.* You attempt to help an individual correct poor workplace habits and return to the agreed-on standard.
Discipline: Verbal and written warnings to change unacceptable behavior.	*Discipline coerces change by warning.* You resort to more forceful measures if the behavior continues despite your efforts to encourage change.
Punish: Punishment is a last resort when other methods fail or when behavior is inappropriate or intolerable.	*Punishment is retaliatory.* You exact reparation from an individual for unacceptable behavior.

Because three of these methods involve documenting a reporter's unsatisfactory behavior, you should keep a note of any reminders you say to an individual in a working binder in case documentation is necessary later. You can also use your notes to remind the individual of conversations.

Practicing and Prompting

Prompting is particularly useful if the problem is an isolated incident or happens infrequently and you don't want to resort to formal disciplinary action. Although you probably won't find practicing and prompting in standard textbooks on supervision, you may want to consider them as particularly applicable in the profession of journalism. Journalists sometimes stretch the rules to accomplish what they consider a greater good—an outstanding story. Editors should take this into consideration.

Counseling, Discipline, and Punishment

When the problem is negligible, you can usually resolve it by simply reminding a reporter of your expectations during a quick conversation. You can reiterate expectations, such as coming to work on time, keeping one's workspace neat, respecting the rights of others, or using equipment properly. You might point out to the reporter that the recent behavior is uncharacteristic—that he or she typically meets expectations. You also want to assure the reporter that this is just a word to the wise, intended to assure a smooth-running newsroom. This kind of conversation is called counseling: it calls attention to behavior that is serious enough to warrant an observation, but not serious enough to record. You should end the brief counseling session with a closing statement such as, "I'm sure this won't happen again."

Formal discipline should be considered when a problem continues despite counseling, and when it adversely affects others, the news report or the company, or the reporter's work. Discipline becomes formal when you tell the reporter that you are taking a disciplinary step and will record it, and you explain the consequences. Discipline is always necessary if the behavior is egregious.

Always document verbal warnings when they are disciplinary rather than counseling reminders. Your organization may also have a policy of requiring several verbal warnings before shifting to a written reprimand. It may require that an employee be suspended (with or without pay) with a written warning.

If you have a collective contract with a union, or your organization has a specific policy, you must follow the rules. Failure to follow the rules in a particular instance will make dealing with behavior problems in others much more difficult. Discipline in your newsroom must be consistent. If you discipline one person more or less than others, you will generate immediate resentment.

Unlike punishment, counseling and discipline work because they imply that you believe the reporter will change. Counseling and discipline are positive and supportive, whereas punishment is retaliatory. Counseling and discipline are designed to change behavior and are progressive. Punishment is designed to exact reparation for inappropriate or unsuitable behavior, and is a one-time event, a last resort.

An Example of Unsatisfactory Behavior

Let's look at an example, the case of a valuable reporter who occasionally fails to meet expectations, since this is the most common newsroom occurrence of unacceptable behavior.

Today is Friday and you're putting together several contributions for an in-depth piece for Sunday's edition. Larry's assignment is the only one missing. Larry was supposed to turn it in on Wednesday, and you had assumed he did. When you call or look for Larry, you find he is not at his desk. You check with personnel and learn he called in sick.

Larry is a veteran journalist. He always has done his job adequately. When you have brought up the subject of late or missed assignments, he has generally corrected his performance and even performs superbly. Whenever Larry is late filing a story he has an ostensibly valid excuse: Interview subjects or sources did not give him enough useful information or didn't answer his messages; he couldn't find the research material he needed; he thought the deadline was different; he was sick.

A verbal, undocumented warning to Larry regarding performance expectations should be enough. Some editors who document verbal warnings normally will dispose of those warnings after a year if the behavior is corrected.

Dealing with Bad Habits

Arriving late for work, loafing, 'Net surfing not related to work, personal e-mailing, or returning suspiciously late from interviews, research, or assignments are fairly common bad habits among reporters. Then there are reporters who arrive on time for work but often waltz in late to meetings or take long breaks, especially after the publication is put to bed or the newscast ends. Habits such as these can be changed. Eminent American psychologist and philosopher William James suggested any habit can be changed in 21 days.[1]

If you feel the reporter has a sincere desire to change a bad habit, whether it is tardiness or some other, here are steps you might suggest.

1. Make a decision to change and begin immediately.
2. Have a sincere and intense desire to change.
3. Replace the bad habit with a new, wholesome habit.
4. Keep constantly alert for opportunities to replace the old with the new habit.
5. Never permit an exception to occur until the new habit has firmly replaced the old.

Changing a habit requires a desire to change. You'll have to make a judgment about the reporter you want to speak to about this. First decide if you want to invest the time and effort needed to convince the individual to change. Here are a few considerations:

- Is this a serious problem or is the bad habit chronic?
- Is work being affected by the habit?
- Are there factors that cause the habit that the reporter can't control?
- Are coworkers affected by this behavior?
- Have there been prior warnings?
- What has been the reporter's response to warnings? Has the reporter continued the unsatisfactory work habit after one or more verbal hints?
- Does the reporter know the consequences of continuing this behavior?
- Did the reporter make a sincere effort to change, followed by a return to the former pattern?

Interviews to counsel a change in a habit require careful planning; they can easily stray from the subject. Because you are pointing out an unsuitable characteristic, this can easily be construed as criticism of the individual and could trigger a communication filter. The reporter might argue with you or block what he or she doesn't want to hear. Therefore, it's important to keep in mind that you are meeting to identify the behavior problem, attempt to determine the cause, encourage a decision to change, and work with the reporter to seek positive alternatives to help resolve the problem. Figure 10.1 on page 126 provides a planning form to help you prepare.

Once you have decided to act, you might ask the reporter to meet informally over coffee for a fact-finding conversation. Begin by mentioning the reporter's bad habit and ask for an explanation. You may discover that the reporter feels the behavior is justified or that it can't be changed. For example, some people find it extremely hard to change their habit of tardiness in spite of repeated efforts. Just about every tardy reporter is keenly aware of late arrivals and would do something about it—if he or she knew what to do. You can help. Schedule a meeting to work with the reporter.

Figure 10.1 Planning a Counseling Interview

Before your meeting, review the reporter's record and make some notes to guide you. Write out a plan for the meeting.

Editor's name: _____ Date: _____

Employee name: _____

What do you want to accomplish? _____
_____

What standard do you expect this reporter to meet? _____
_____

Does the reporter know the standard?   ❏ Yes   ❏ No

Have you mentioned this problem to the reporter before?   ❏ Yes   ❏ No

When and how? _____

What examples do you have to prove that the standard is not being met? What specific standard has been broken?

(Write down specific instances describing the behavior, or work that was not done, or not done in a specific way, or dates of tardiness. Use this list when you meet to provide examples of failure to meet standards.)

Example _____ Date _____

Example _____ Date _____

Example _____ Date _____

Example _____ Date _____

Example _____ Date _____

Example _____ Date _____

What do you expect the change in behavior to be? _____
_____
_____

Performance appraisal sessions are an excellent time for this. Your comments should be pro-active rather than reactive during the meeting. Pro-active comments focus on solutions; reactive comments focus on criticism or accusation. For example, comments such as "You need to work more quickly" or "You have a negative outlook" are critical rather than pro-active.

Be inclusive rather than exclusive; talk in terms of how "we" (the journalists in the newsroom and the company) are affected by the behavior rather than in terms of how "you" should change. Explain how the behavior affects news production, potential for raises, company profits, recognition for superior work, and newsroom morale among coworkers who also contribute to the same goals. Sometimes these reminders are enough to motivate people who hadn't seen their job as a career that contributes to a network and helps the company grow and expand.

To get more information on how the reporter views the bad habit, ask questions such as "Is there something I should know that causes you to arrive late to work or to return late from breaks?" and "Are there factors that are beyond your control that affect arriving on time?" Ask the reporter to describe those factors and write down the details. Then ask what you can do to help the reporter find a solution. Solutions that the reporter generates are more likely to be acted on than those that you impose. People will put extra pressure on themselves when the solution was their idea. Another problem you face when you impose your own solution is that the reporter may argue that your remedy is not possible. "I would have done that long ago if it hadn't been for . . ." the reporter can counter. Or "If only so-and-so would do her job more quickly, I wouldn't have this problem."

Some reporters can be surprisingly creative in the way they react to, resist, or even refuse to change. If you're not careful, you can get into an argument about the solution. Remember that you're not negotiating—you're seeking a decision to change.

Discussing a Need to Change

You may discover that the reporter is unaware of a habit that causes poor performance. Unsatisfactory work habits can be a result of learned behavior. The reporter may unconsciously be mimicking others—parents, other reporters, or former editors—and might reveal this in a conversation: "That's the way I learned to do it," or, "That's how we did it at the last place I worked." Sometimes, correcting bad habits is that simple—discovering their source and correcting the reporter's perception. An explanation of why the behavior is unacceptable coupled with a mutually satisfactory plan to change it may be all that is needed.

Reaching Agreement to Change

During your meeting, point out that four steps are essential to change a habit.

1. The reporter must know the consequences if the behavior does not change.
2. The reporter must make a decision to change.
3. The reporter must make a plan to substitute different behavior for the present behavior.
4. The reporter must carry out the plan with a consistent effort.

After the reporter has agreed to change, help the reporter work out a plan. Make sure it is specific. Rather than settling for a broad statement such as "I'll try harder," write down ways to measure the reporter's growth. Establish milestones to measure progress. As an example, if the reporter arrives only a few minutes late, set a goal for early arrival every day for one week. Then expand that to two and finally to four weeks in a row. Mark your calendar to review results in a month.

Before the reporter leaves, reaffirm your confidence and assure the reporter that you will continue to offer support.

Dealing with Personal Problems

Problems not related to work can affect performance. Family or other personal problems can cause people to worry excessively, take personal problems into the workplace, misunderstand or make false assumptions about events or comments by others, and even create problems for others in the newsroom. Personal financial problems, for example, can cause a reporter to reach unrealistic conclusions about salary or the amount of a raise, or how often the reporter is entitled to one. These can affect performance. People are not always aware that such problems are distracting them in their work.

If you discover that a personal problem is affecting a reporter's performance, treat it confidentially. When personal problems cause work problems, you'll want to listen—and help if you can—without appearing to be prying. Information about a personal problem should not go into the reporter's file, nor should you share it with other editors or the reporter's colleagues.

Approach personal problems in a spirit of a compassionate listener rather than omniscient problem-solver. Editors are not marriage counselors or psychologists, nor are they expected to be. Employees who share a personal problem with the boss are often grateful the boss took the time just to listen. You should not feel you are expected to take the problem on your shoulders simply because it was brought to you. Nor should failure to solve a personal problem mean that the conversation about it was a failure. Your best response in such situations is to listen without offering advice. However, if the problem is something within your power to resolve, you may pitch in and do what you can as a sympathetic supervisor.

Verbal Warnings

Take immediate disciplinary action when it is required; you shouldn't store up too many examples before you take action. If you do, you may be implying consent.

If unsatisfactory performance continues after counseling, meet formally with the reporter as soon as you can after the most recent occurrence of the problem and take the following steps:

1. State the problem and review your organization's standards.
2. Provide specific examples of how the standards are not being met, including dates and times. Make sure the reporter understands what rules were broken.
3. Point out that performance has not improved.
4. Advise the reporter that you are issuing a verbal warning and are placing a note in the reporter's file.
5. Offer the reporter the opportunity to review and sign the document. Some organizations encourage this; others require it. The purpose of signing the warning is not to request that the reporter agree with it but only to show that the reporter received the warning.
6. Establish a trial period during which change should occur.
7. Explain the consequences if the unsatisfactory performance continues.
8. Ask if there is anything the company can do to help.

An attorney who asked to remain anonymous suggests that step 8 should be your last statement in the meeting. It is an extremely important question because you are giving the reporter an opportunity to reveal anything that might prevent compliance. The attorney also advises that you make sure you document the fact that you asked this question, whether or not there was a reply.

As you review performance during the trial period, be sure to mention that you notice positive change. If a reporter makes an effort to correct the problem after it has been documented, be sure to record the effort to change and the positive results. It is unfair to the reporter to record only poor performance without balancing that information with records when the reporter has made efforts to improve.

The reporter can be put on probation for a specific period, usually 30 days with a maximum of 90 days, then evaluated at the end of that period.

If verbal warnings fail, discipline is your next option. Avoid getting into arguments with the reporter when you discipline. If the reporter gets you angry, walk away until you cool off. Be careful to avoid acting emotionally; it would not be fair to suspend a reporter for a single tardy arrival because you lost your temper.

Behaviors that warrant discipline are listed in Table 10.2.

Written Warnings

A written warning is serious. It goes into the employee's record. You must conduct a meeting to advise a reporter of a written warning. Start the meeting with examples of the behavior, comparing them against standards. Review the consequences of continuing the unsatisfactory performance with the reporter and explain that a record of each warning will form part of the reporter's personnel record. Tell the reporter that, if standards are not met within a certain period, you will issue a final warning. Write out a formal report of the meeting and ask the reporter to sign it.[2]

Termination

If the reporter ignores written warnings or flagrantly violates norms and standards, the reporter's employment should be terminated.[3] How do you decide whether firing is indicated? First, the punishment should be equal to the violation. Second, the cause for firing should be something that is spelled out in the personnel manual.

You must be consistent: Apply the same standards to every individual in the same way. This is essential to show uniformity in treatment of every individual if the reporter decides to challenge the firing in court. By the time you reach the stage where termination of a reporter is your only option, you should be prepared to prove your case for dismissal. You should have plenty of documentation to show the reporter failed to perform adequately or did not respond to discipline. Thorough documentation helps protect your organization against legal action. This is why it is so important to begin a record at the first sign of difficulty and maintain it throughout the entire employment period. Additionally, you must be certain that the record will show the reporter was treated fairly and given the same treatment as everyone else in your organization.

When you are convinced that your only recourse is to fire an individual, consult with legal counsel, the human resources director, and your superior. Given the changes in legislation and the differences in the law

Table 10.2 Behaviors That Would Lead to Disciplinary Action

A list of types of conduct which may result in a reporter receiving discipline (in accordance with company policy) and up to termination, listed alphabetically, would include:

1. Criminal conviction
2. Failure to notify of absence according to department policy
3. Failure to report for work for three days without calling in
4. Gambling on company property
5. Gross misconduct or behavior on or off company property
6. Habitual absenteeism or tardiness
7. Inappropriate appearance
8. Inappropriate manner reflected in tone of voice, or rudeness
9. Incompetent job performance
10. Insubordination or refusal to accept a work assignment
11. Intentionally jeopardizing health, safety, or property of other staff, visitors, or company
12. Making intentionally false or derogatory statements concerning the organization's facilities, services, or programs, or one's colleagues
13. Offensive behavior toward employees of the same or opposite sex, even if the offense was never reported to management
14. Possession of weapons on company property
15. Soliciting or accepting gratuities or gifts in exchange for writing a story
16. Theft of company or personal property
17. Breach of confidentiality
18. Unlawful possession, manufacture, distribution, dispensing, sale, or use of alcohol or drugs
19. Unprofessional behavior or inappropriate conduct that could result in bodily harm, is of an intimate nature, or is disruptive to conducting business
20. Use of abusive language or language disruptive to conducting business in the newsroom
21. Violation of company rules and policies
22. Violation of safety or fire rules

from state to state, and federal law, you should not take any action on your own. Human resources personnel are being called on increasingly either to handle the termination or to be present when a reporter is notified of termination. The human resources department will provide information for the employee on such issues as final paycheck, surrender of equipment and keys or security passes, monies due the company or the employee, and other matters.

As an effective editor, you should not put off disciplinary action when it is required. Not only is discipline an essential element of every editor's responsibilities, it is an essential element of any quality personnel program.

You selected your staff; most will work well and diligently, never causing disciplinary action. On the contrary, you will want to help them grow in their jobs. In the next chapter we look at conducting an annual performance appraisal. During the year you discuss your expectations; in the performance review you document them.

Notes

1. The suggested steps are based on William James' five rules to change a habit. Here are the rules as James wrote them in Chapter 6, *Habit,* pages 123–131, from *The Works of William James, The Principles of Psychology,* Harvard University Press, 1981. His rules appear in the text in italics.

Launch ourselves with as strong and decided an initiative as possible. Never suffer an exception to occur till the new habit is securely rooted in your life. Seize the very first possible opportunity to act on every resolution you make, and on every emotional prompting you may experience in the direction of the habits you aspire to gain. Don't preach too much to your pupils or abound in good talk in the abstract. Keep the faculty of effort alive in you by a little gratuitous exercise every day.

2. Your organization may have a progressive discipline policy as well as policies for grievance and arbitration. Ask your legal counsel or human resources director to explain them to you.

3. This suggested guide to plan and conduct employee terminations is not intended to nor provides advice regarding legal ramifications. Readers are encouraged to consult with legal counsel with respect to these issues.

# SECTION FOUR

Coaching

11 Conducting Performance Appraisal Interviews

After you finish this chapter, you will be able to:
- Plan a performance appraisal
- Conduct a performance appraisal
- Put a reporter at ease during the interview
- Help a reporter set goals to improve performance

Introduction

Not much time is left in a busy day for an unhurried and in-depth discussion with reporters about where they are doing well in their jobs and where they could improve. Yet they have a right to know. Moreover, you could use some feedback on how reporters in your newsroom perceive both their jobs and their contribution to the news report. So it makes sense to set aside some time for such an assessment. The best time for this is during a performance review, which benefits you as well as reporters.

This session should be both instructive and gratifying, since it can help your reporters stretch. Yet many reporters and editors seem to have a universal dislike for performance reviews. Editors who don't like spending time on a performance review will postpone it, then rush through it. Some reporters may be reluctant to prepare for the review because they assume the outcome has been predetermined. Others suspect that you are just going through the motions to justify a decision you have already made about a raise, for example.

The performance appraisal is a valuable tool for both you and your staff and far too important to be disdained. During the year you have discussed your expectations; now in the performance review you document them.

Planning a Performance Appraisal Interview

During the performance appraisal you can provide information the reporter needs to perform to the best of his or her ability. You can also take the opportunity to recognize the reporter's outstanding achievement in meeting your expectations and identify areas where improvement is required. This objective ought to be clear to the reporter, who should know ahead of time that you have prepared for the interview. The candidate should know why you are getting together and even make plans to discuss points he or she would like to cover during the interview.

Although you may feel that some of the reporters in your newsroom could stand improvement, rare is the reporter who thinks he or she is *not* doing a good job. (If you doubt this, just ask any reporter, "Do you think you're doing a bad job?") Because reporters are confident that they're doing a good job, their self-assessment may be substantially different from yours.

Here's an example. An excellent writer was reassigned from covering a beat to rewriting copy from other reporters on the same beat. Although he was a fine writer, he had to develop skills to deal with the volume of copy and deadlines in the new position. The editor's plan was for the writer to develop and grow. The writer did well during the first couple of months but gradually began to lose direction, and his work suffered. A grade system was used to evaluate the writer's performance at a six-month review. The editor graded the performance and the writer did the same on a separate form. Each filled in quite different evaluations in every category on a scale of one to five. The writer's evaluation was much higher than the editor's.

Typically, you would ask a reporter to fill out a self-assessment or reporter input form prior to the appraisal review, but this is optional. Give the form to the reporter about a week ahead of the session. This allows the individual plenty of opportunity to prepare any questions or points for discussion of specific issues. It also encourages the reporter to participate actively, which is important since you are talking about the reporter's future as well as the past.

At the same time you should fill out your own assessment form, on which you evaluate the reporter's work (see Figure 11.1). Do it well in advance of the session—the reporter has a right to your thoughtful consideration. Although you will discuss both the reporter's and your evaluations, yours is the only copy you should file in the reporter's record. The reporter should review and sign your evaluation and receive a copy. The signature only verifies that the individual reviewed the report; it

Figure 11.1 Performance Appraisal

Reporter Self-Evaluation for Performance Review

This form has been designed to provide information and perspective for your editor for use in performance review and discussion. Write in your comments regarding any or all of the following performance criteria. Provide concrete examples. Make an effort to avoid being subjective.

- Performance relative to goals
- Adherence to policies and procedures
- Relations with colleagues and others
- Maintenance and enhancement of professional skills
- Maintenance and enhancement of technical skills
- Teamwork
- Other (specify) _____

Comments: _____

_____
_____
_____
_____
_____
_____
_____
_____

Name _____

Signature _____

Date _____

Please return this form to _____ before _____ (date).

does not necessarily mean agreement. Allow the reporter to add comments about the report.

Performance appraisals offer an opportunity to provide guidance to employees on their careers, encouraging and motivating them and even providing recognition, so they should not be rushed. On the other hand, if you have been providing regular input to your staff, the performance appraisal should not take longer than fifteen minutes and there won't be any surprises.

Conducting a Performance Appraisal Interview

Since a performance appraisal is a session some reporters view with apprehension, it's important to ease the reporter's anxiety at the outset to make your sessions both productive and meaningful. Reporters should be keenly aware that this is an opportunity to find out how they are doing and where they are going.

You can reduce psychological barriers by conducting the interview in two chairs with no furniture between you. Place both chairs in front of your desk or on the same side of a table. This promotes a feeling of openness. Put the employee at ease with small talk for a few minutes as you begin, but remain business-like rather than friendly throughout the session.

When you feel the reporter is ready, spell out the items to be discussed. Let him or her know that the purpose of the performance appraisal is to motivate performance improvement rather than to punish failures or shortcomings. The appraisal interview should not be confused with a meeting to change unsatisfactory behavior.

Next chronicle what the reporter does well. Conflict can arise and cast a pall over the rest of the session if you start listing what was not done, or done wrong, or what needs to change. One technique for keeping the interview positive is to ask if the reporter would especially like to discuss a particular matter right away. This helps you target areas of concern at the outset. Reporters find this especially helpful if there is a specific question or topic they have been wondering about. If you don't ask, the reporter might not pay attention to anything else you have to say until that topic is discussed. It's a good idea to bring it up immediately and then continue with the other items that you want to cover.

New reporters may not have questions or comments at the outset since they won't know what to expect. They may want to hear first what you have to say about their performance before making any comments, so get right to the point after you've given the reporter a chance to bring up any special topic.

After summarizing what the reporter has been doing well, review the reporter's self-assessment. This is especially valuable since you can get a frank opinion about the job as well as how the reporter sees himself or herself in it. You may find out that the reporter's idea of the job is distinct from yours. Ask the reporter to comment on the self-assessment. As you listen to the reporter's analysis, silently compare your views with the reporter's.

Now you can discuss where the reporter can improve, but be careful you don't let the conversation become a monologue. You want the reporter to contribute. Make sure the reporter participates as much as possible in the discussion. If you don't, the reporter may think you don't really care about his or her point of view, possibly because you have already passed judgment. Keep encouraging the reporter to contribute thoughts and comments throughout the interview. If the reporter has views that conflict with yours, make sure the reporter's count as much as yours.

Focus on the future and how the reporter can improve even when you talk about past performance. Point out areas where the reporter can make changes for the better. The employee may want to explain to you why the behavior you've pointed out is difficult to change. Don't dismiss this input. This is your chance to learn how the reporter views the job and find out about any difficulties you may not be aware of. Listen carefully so that you can offer any solutions. For example, let's say the reporter comes back late from lunch often. By providing the reporter an opportunity to explain, you might discover that this person calls to check with daycare each day and is often put on hold for extended periods. Or the reporter might use an occasional lunch hour to visit an elderly or dependent relative.

Be prepared for opposition of another kind. The reporter may take the attitude that this is just an opportunity on your part to criticize and may not accept much of what you say. Or the reporter may counter with an argument that your expectations are far greater than any one person could fulfill. The reporter can come up with a variety of justifications or simply blame the company or colleagues. If this happens, you may find out more about this reporter than you had planned to. You'll learn that the reporter has a problem accepting positive criticism. There is not a whole lot you can do about that.

Before you end the interview, ask the reporter to tell you about anything he or she is doing well that has gone unnoticed.

Many reporters will listen and say, "Yes, sir," or "Yes, ma'am," to the boss to get the performance appraisal over with in order to get back to work. Others may remain silent because they simply disagree. You may not find out how the reporter felt about the appraisal interview until much later. If you suspect the reporter may not agree with your assessments, ask for his or her input and take time to discuss it. You're not looking for approval; you are asking for commitment. Enthusiastic commitment is always better than resigned acceptance, even if it takes longer to accomplish.

Setting Goals

Before you end the performance appraisal, encourage the reporter to plan short- and long-term goals. Long-term goals focus on the future: training, growth, development, and the reporter's place in your organization. Short-term goals focus on the present. Encourage the reporter to suggest ways he or she can achieve these goals.

As you plan both short- and long-term goals together, your responsibility is to guide the reporter to do well in the present so that he or she can take better advantage of opportunities as they become available. Point out to the reporter how important it is to work with a passion for excellence now, in order to be well positioned for consideration for opportunities in the future. You may find it helpful to use the forms in Figures 11.2, 11.3, and 11.4.

If you summarize the interview, make sure you clarify anything that might have confused the reporter. Restate any agreements for corrective action. Make clear that the reporter is ultimately responsible for growth. The reporter must know what the company can and cannot do. Compliment the employee on his or her strengths once more, briefly review your expectations, and then write your documentation before you proceed to conduct an appraisal of the next reporter.

To practice all the supervisory duties discussed so far, as well as fulfill your editing responsibilities, you'll need to make every minute of every day productive. This is why developing your skill at managing your time effectively is so important. If you often complain you don't have enough time in the day to accomplish everything you have to do, look at the suggestions in the next chapter on time management, for both you and your staff.

Figure 11.2 Performance Appraisal

Editor's Form

Reporter Name _____

Position _____

Primary Work Area _____

Immediate Superior (if applicable) _____

Date _____

Conducting Performance Appraisal Interviews

General	Yes	No	NA	Comments
Punctuality				
Telephone etiquette (courtesy; identifies self, department)				
Adheres to dress code				
Respects rights of all colleagues				
Demonstrates compliance with mandatory regulations				
Understands and complies with safety regulations				
Knows organization's mission statement				
Other				

Organization/Rights/Ethics	1	2	3	4	5	NA	Comments
Interacts appropriately with colleagues							
Interacts appropriately with superiors							
Maintains confidentiality							
Demonstrates knowledge of job							
Demonstrates creativity in writing or production							
Demonstrates initiative							
Interacts appropriately with persons outside organization							

The numbers refer to the Code on the next page. Check the one that applies.

(continued)

(continued)

CODE

Performance Level	Performance Expectation
1	Consistently displays behavior and performance above expectations
2	Occasionally displays behavior and performance above expectations
3	Meets expectations on a regular basis
4	Occasionally displays behavior and performance that is below expectations
5	Performance and behavior are below expectations consistently; needs to improve performance level to retain position with the organization

Additional Comments _____

Ability to think creatively _____

Writing ability _____

Interviewing ability _____

Ability to handle new technology _____

Reporter's Signature _____

Editor's Signature _____

Date _____

Figure 11.3 Reporter's Five-Step Plan to Set Goals to Improve Performance

Step I

Distinguish your long-range goals from short-term goals. Long-range goals will take longer than a year to achieve; short-term goals can be accomplished during the next 12 months. Write up to five top long-range and five short-range goals below.

Long-Range Goals

1. _____
2. _____
3. _____
4. _____
5. _____

(Use more space for additional goals.)

Short-Range Goals

1. _____
2. _____
3. _____
4. _____
5. _____

(Use more space for additional goals.)

Step II

Select the short-term goal that is most important to you and write it below.

1. _____

Step III

List the rest of the goals in order of importance.

2. _____
3. _____
4. _____
5. _____

Step IV

Identify and write down the obstacles you will have to overcome to achieve your primary short-term goal, selected in Step II.

_____
_____
_____
_____

Figure 11.4 Establish a time frame to achieve your goals

Write in the most important short-term goal here 1. _____	Start date (Today)	Target date (Not more than 90 days Date: _____	Check when attained ☑
(Write in the rest of the goals here in order of importance.) 2. _____			
3. _____			
4. _____			
5. _____			
(Use extra space if you have more goals.) Write in the most important long-term goal here 1. _____		Target date (One year or more) Date: _____	
(Write in the rest of the long-term goals here in order of importance.) 2. _____			
3. _____			
4. _____			
5. _____			
(Use extra space if you have more goals.)			

12 Time Management for You and Your Staff

After you finish this chapter, you will be able to:
- Analyze and log how you use your time
- Trace the causes of poor time management
- Distinguish the important from the urgent
- Improve time management in the newsroom

Introduction

"Each of us already has all the time there is," time management expert R. Alec Mackenzie points out. "Few people have enough; yet everyone has all there is."[1]

New technology promises you will accomplish more in less time. That's the theory, anyway. Planners, hand-held electronic marvels, Web portals to manage your calendar, voice recognition, wireless communication, and time management software are all designed to increase productivity by organizing your days, hours and minutes. Yet technology has produced more activities to do, not more time to do them in. Calls, e-mail, and faxes multiply faster than anyone can handle them. Many editors throw up their hands in despair. Do any of the following sound familiar?

- You feel overwhelmed.
- You feel you are always behind in your work.
- You often postpone tough or complex tasks.
- You are busy but feel you are not doing the right things.
- You leave your place of work exhausted but no further ahead.
- You have missed an important family event.

What editors can't keep up with are new forms of urgent communication that delay taking care of the truly important. Which will get your priority attention, for example, a reporter at your door, a fax marked urgent, a blinking e-mail message on your digital screen, or the telephone, when all are clamoring simultaneously?

Do you often feel you can't control your time either because of the demands of others or because of other external forces? Two forces influence your time: external and internal. Poor daily planning is an internal force. Failure to control internal forces often results from lack of knowledge of time management methods or even awareness of them, failure to maintain rigorous time management discipline, or simply failure to recognize that demand for your attention is a time management issue.

Actually, the term *time management* is a misnomer. No one can manage time: It marches inexorably on, no matter how hard you try to control it. What you can do is manage the tasks you have to do in the time you have available. You do this by rigorously planning your day. Many editors disdain a pocket planner or an electronic personal information manager. Some people work best with these popular tools, but others find them distracting, time-consuming, even counterproductive. You may be one of those editors who can't see the merit in spending 10 minutes or so every morning to maintain a detailed work diary. Or you may be an editor who conscientiously records pending tasks according to priority but never gets to those at the bottom of the list, merely copying them day after week after month, until they are eventually obsolete.

How You Use Your Time

Time Usage Analysis Number One

Here's a useful method to analyze your time use. The following is a list of a typical editor's daily activities. All of the activities have been imposed by others, rather than determined by the editor. Review the list and check all those that apply to you during a typical day:

- Telephone calls
- Interruptions
- Meetings
- Handling reader enquiries
- Visits by staff (scheduled and nonscheduled)
- Writing messages to correct or change copy

- Rewriting copy
- Rewriting heads, captions, and editing
- Personnel problems
- Putting out fires

Now ask yourself whether you manage your time or time manages you. List what you consider to be your four major time wasters:

1. _____
2. _____
3. _____
4. _____

If you are like most editors, you listed telephone calls and "telephone tag," meetings, drop-in visitors, and delays caused by others.

However, after an analysis of their own days, many editors find a new list of time wasters. Most are generated by themselves: doing tasks that others should do, dealing with crises, lack of a plan for the day, allowing anyone to interrupt for often frivolous reasons, and procrastinating. Here are 15 more ways that editors waste time. Check those that apply to you:

- Searching for files in the office or computer
- Taking too long to edit stories
- Taking too long to assign stories
- Taking too long to select pictures or art
- Putting off important tasks until they become crises
- Repeating instructions due to poor communication
- Failing to finish tasks
- Attempting to accomplish too much
- Inflated expectations of others
- Theorizing endlessly with others about interesting stories
- Making unnecessary trips into the newsroom
- Looking for information you know you put down somewhere
- Redoing something you didn't do right the first time
- Viewing or reading far too much of the competition or for far too many hours
- Surfing the Web following interesting links that turn into dead ends

Next, track your own day with a time log. A time log will help you:

- Analyze how you allocate your time
- Analyze your list of tasks for the day
- Analyze your ability to control the activities you choose to carry out

Conduct two analyses of your use of time. Do the first one now. This analysis looks at how you spend your day and how you perceive your time is controlled by impositions of others. Put into practice the tips you learn in this chapter. After six months, analyze how you spend your day again. You should notice a significant improvement, especially in how you have improved in the 20 ways that editors waste time.

TIME LOG

It's essential that you log your use of your time. Many editors who attend time management classes walk out thinking they will waste their time trying to measure their use of it. But the fact is you can't correct what you are doing unless you know what you are doing.

One objection editors have is that a time log is too involved, requiring a record every 15 minutes for a week or two. Yours needn't be so detailed. As a matter of fact, a time log must be easy and quick to do or you won't take the time to do it. To make logging painless, use a code to record frequent activities; you will only need a second to check off each item daily. A sample code to record your typical daily activities appears in Figure 12.1.

Figure 12.1 Time Log

How to use this time log:

1. *Record.* Every 15 minutes, write in a one-letter category code.
2. *Add.* At the end of each day, add up the minutes and then fill in the Total Time Spent On box. You may also want to calculate the percentage.
3. *Review.* Keep the log for a week (two weeks is better) and at the end of each week total the amount and percentage of time you spend on each category.
4. *Analyze.* Examine how you spend your time each week. Notice how much work is repetitive. Ask yourself which items could be improved. For example, which phone calls could have been briefer? Which visits could have been shortened?
5. *Design.* Using your analysis, plan a strategy to improve how you use your time and stick to it.

Time Log

	MON.	TUES.	WED.	THURS.	FRI.	SAT.	SUN.
7 a.m.							
8 a.m.							
9 a.m.							
10 a.m.							
11 a.m.							
Noon							
1 p.m.							
2 p.m.							
3 p.m.							
4 p.m.							
5 p.m.							
6 p.m.							
7 p.m.							
8 p.m.							
9 p.m.							
10 p.m.							
11 p.m.							
12 a.m.							
1 a.m.							
2 a.m.							
3 a.m.							
4 a.m.							
5 a.m.							
6 a.m.							

Weekly Time Log

CATEGORY	MON.	TUES.	WED.	THURS.	FRI.	SAT.	SUN.	SYNOPSIS TOTAL TIME SPENT ON	% OF WEEK
Telephone									
Meetings									
Editing									
Communicating									
Writing									
Visitors									
Other									
Other									

T = Telephone; M = Meetings; E = Editing; C = Communicate (messages, etc.); W = Writing;
V = Visitors; O = Other.

Finding the Causes of Poor Time Management

Editors who routinely reach the end of the workday wondering where the time went probably are unaware of the source of their time management problems. What do you think are the sources of poor time management? Write in your answers:

_____

Sometimes the source is simply a lifetime habit of managing time poorly. Often, however, time management difficulties can also be traced to behavior. The best approach to improving time management depends on an individual's behavioral style.

The test in Figure 12.2 will help you look at how you react to events. Scoring: 0–14 is Acceptable; 15-29 means your time management is Adequate; 30–40 is an Alert to improve.

Figure 12.2 Behavior Test

Check the number that most closely represents your normal behavior. 0 = Never; N = Not me; O = Occassionally; F = Frequently; T = That's me

	N 1	O 2	F 3	T 4
1. I closely monitor the news rather than relax on days off.				
2. I don't watch the time and end up dashing from one place to another or from one meeting to another.				
3. I can be impatient with people who don't understand something quickly.				
4. I feel out of control when I'm away from the newsroom.				
5. People who are important to me don't get enough of my time.				
6. I often do a task myself when I should delegate it.				
7. I skip lunch or eat meals at my desk.				
8. I would rather work than spend break time with colleagues.				
9. When I'm working on one assignment, I can get distracted and fret about a different thing.				
10. The deadline environment energizes me.				
Add the numbers in each column				
Write in your total score				

Acceptable means you handle time relatively well. Adequate means you could improve. Alert means you need to pay immediate attention to improving your time management.

Time Usage Analysis Number Two

Editors are often unaware that time is wasted in two ways: by those who interrupt and by the editors themselves. Now that you have completed your time log, review the following list and check all the ways you use your time during the day in addition to those you checked in Time Usage Analysis Number One. Look for internal factors; that is, time wasters that you are responsible for.

- Organizing poorly
- Not letting others do their job (doing the job yourself because it's faster or easier)
- Engaging in activities not directly related to work (personal, professional associations, committees)
- Not listening carefully
- Trying to do too much at once
- Making unrealistic estimates of how long each task or activity will take
- Putting things off
- Failing to say no
- Involving too many people in a meeting, project, or planning session
- Making decisions too quickly

What should become evident is that many of your problems with time usage during the day are self-generated. True time management can only begin when you admit this and decide to do something about it.

Distinguishing the Important from the Urgent

Urgent matters get immediate attention. They are not, however, always the activities you should be spending your time on at any given moment during the day. Urgent matters often turn out to be time wasters and rob you of precious minutes you need to accomplish your important daily work. More than ever before, successful time management in the new media workplace depends on

- How well you distinguish between the urgent and the important
- How well you move forward on important issues while successfully managing urgent issues

Following are 12 tips to help you manage both simultaneously.

Control

Work on both urgent and important matters in blocks of time. Spend ten minutes on an important task during an hour when you're handling an urgent matter (a breaking story, for example). By dedicating a specific block of time to a task that has to be finished while you are managing an urgent matter, you can work on both the urgent and the important in any one-hour period. But give your full attention to only one at a time.

Evaluate

Before you even begin, ask yourself what might happen if you postpone an urgent task (for example, answering an urgent e-mail or responding to a drop-in visitor immediately). What would be the consequences? Can you delay the task until after you have completed your present important task?

Reject

Learn how to say no. Every time you accept a project someone else hands you, you admit that your own work is not as important as the task given you by others. Ironically, you're sending a message that you are not as busy as the other person is.

Recommend

Can someone else handle this? The best use of your time is to accomplish those tasks you do well and let others handle jobs they should be responsible for. Suggest someone else, a shortcut, or another way to do it to those who interrupt or make demands on your time. Establish the perception that you are busy and have plenty to do, and that adding another task is a serious proposition. Make it apparent that your day is planned. It may be ego-pleasing to take on a task another can't handle, but if it alters your schedule, your own work will suffer.

Assess

The time it takes to do something usually turns out to be longer than you anticipated. Most tasks take longer than you may initially estimate because of interruptions, distractions, or failure of others to do their part as expected. To more accurately estimate the time it will take to complete a task and avoid unrealistic appraisals, add 15 minutes to an hour to any estimate, depending on the complexity of a specific task.

Organize

Unorganized stacks on the desk and the floor, a poor filing system, and pending projects staring at you can stifle the best intentions to manage time efficiently. Experts suggest that you work on only one project at a time. That way, you would have only one piece of work on your desk or screen at a time. While this may be an attractive theory, editors regularly work on several tasks simultaneously. The trick to managing several projects at the same time is to decide at the outset which one will get your primary attention, and then categorize all others in descending order—and stick to your plan until you have finished.

Manage

Keep your workspace neat. Never let more than two piles accumulate on your desk at one time: work to do right now and future work. If you have more than two stacks, you are taking on more than you can handle or failing to finish enough current work.

Improve

Modify your filing system. You may have an excellent system but fail to keep it current, dump papers in wrong files, or otherwise misuse the system. A superb filing system has three requirements:

- Each item has a place
- Each item is filed in a timely manner
- Each item can be found when you need it

Discard

Keep files clear of clutter. Set a time limit for keeping materials. Throw out anything you haven't needed after a certain period—for example 18 months. Journalists accumulate staggering hoards of reports, background material, studies, business cards, copies, printouts, downloads, floppies, and CDs that were useful only once, are dated, or are from sources who are no longer in the field. Keep only what you need (including for legal reasons).

Document

Maintain a to-do list and respect it. Employ a priority system and mark each item on the list (from one to three). A to-do list helps you remember tasks, protects you from procrastination, and serves as a record of accomplishments.

Combat

Fight the journalist's fatal drop-in visitor addiction. Is there a reason people feel that they can interrupt you at will? Does your desk face the door so that anyone can catch your eye? Do you have an inviting vacant chair in your office? Do you look out of your office at people going by, perhaps catching their eye with an inviting glance? Do you combine socializing with work-related topics when you talk to reporters?

When a drop-in visitor plops down in a chair unannounced and asks, "Got a minute?" say, "I'm busy with this important task and must finish it immediately. Can we meet later?" Better yet, get up from your chair and deal with the issue while both of you are standing. When you finish, take the visitor by the arm and walk together toward the door to your office, finishing the conversation and directing the person out of the office. Then turn your back, alone, and return to your chair.

Respect

Treat the telephone the way you would treat a drop-in visitor if you were in conference with someone in your office. If you are busy, let the call transfer to voice mail. Handle messages in segments of time after you finish your tasks. You can always interrupt your task if the caller's business is important—the caller's message will alert you to that.

Compress

Keep telephone conversations brief. It's easy to add socializing to a business call and lose precious minutes. Monitor your time on the phone: Notice when the call begins and set a limit for yourself. Look at telephone conversation this way: Just four 15-minute telephone conversations can rob you of one-fourth of your morning.

List Important Tasks

As you begin each day, make a list of important tasks and schedule them first. Use a form such as the one in Figure 12.3. Write in urgent tasks and

Figure 12.3 Daily Plan

	TODAY	SHORT RANGE	LONG RANGE
Important			
Urgent			

leave space for any that may come up during the day. Schedule your important tasks first, then schedule the urgent tasks. Rather than answer e-mail messages and phone calls as they come in, batch them into a specific interval and spend 15 to 20 minutes replying. The key to success is to stick to your daily plan.

Improving Time Management in Your Newsroom

As a leader, you should help those who report to you to manage their time. Efficient time management in the newsroom will produce more, and better stories at a lower cost. While the need for time management is obvious to you as an editor, it may be much less of a priority for reporters.

Here are some protests you might hear:

- "I can't get my regular work done because you continuously assign me huge projects."
- "Quality takes time."
- "I try to manage my time, but I never seem to have enough time during the day for everything. The day just gets away from me."

Your reporters may have concluded that time management is something only management practices (meaning editors must manage time but reporters, producers, or broadcast news personnel don't have to). Nevertheless, because demands on time will only increase in the new media workplace, effective time management is not a choice; it's a critical skill that everyone in the newsroom should practice. Make sure reporters understand that time management is everyone's responsibility, not just management's.

Reporters are less likely to take offense at frequent reminders to remain on schedule and manage time conscientiously if all of you agree in advance about its importance. Spend a few minutes with your staff discussing the advantages of efficient time management. Ask them for examples of how they think time is wasted in their workplace. Most time wasters in today's newsrooms can be traced to one of two sources:

- factors outside of the newsroom
- reporters, producers, or broadcast news personnel themselves

Table 12.1 gives some examples of newsroom time wasters and solutions.

Take it upon yourself to make sure time management gets as much attention as the most important story you are working on. In the final analysis, that's how you'll make sure that story you are working on is well written.

As you and your staff become more adept at managing time, you will accomplish more in less time and as a result enhance productivity, one of your key goals as a manager. Coaching is also an excellent way to help each person on your staff reach maximum potential. In the next chapter you'll learn when to coach, how to coach, and what to include in a coaching session.

Notes

1. *The Time Trap Managing Your Way Out,* R. Alec Mackenzie, AMACOM, 3rd Edition, 1997.

Table 12.1 Newsroom Time Wasters and Solutions

TIME WASTER	POSSIBLE CAUSE	SOLUTION
Socializing with visitors	Personal visits by friends or others that distract reporters.	Screen unscheduled visitors at the front desk.
Socializing among reporters and inefficiency	Activities unrelated to work, such as gossip, trips for coffee or sodas, or reading too many publications looking for leads, discussing an interesting story. Research shows that reporters can spend as much as four out of eight hours of every day on such activities, which become so habitual that they develop into ritual and consequently seem essential.	Interrupt the conversation and assign stories since socializing reporters don't seem to have enough work.
Delay in filing a story	In order to proceed, the individual has to wait for others to deliver work or complete essential tasks.	Create a spirit of teamwork and awareness of the importance of everyone's job among newsroom staff.
Missing information	Reporters, producers or broadcast news personnel may misfile, not file, or fail to file reports, copies of letters, schedules, clips, diskettes, CDs, or other information in a timely manner. They may also have a poor filing system in their data files.	Develop an easy-to-understand newsroom-wide electronic filing system and insist that all reporters adhere to it.

(continued)

Time Waster	Possible Cause	Solution
Starting several tasks, or switching among tasks without fully completing any because of unrealistic estimates of time required to complete a story or project	Reporters may fail to plan a story before they begin, then waste precious time searching for data or making unnecessary extra phone calls. The reporter may be unfamiliar with or new to the beat.	Coach reporters to plan a story and research for essential information before they begin. Discuss the problem with the reporter to determine the reason, then help the reporter improve how time is managed. The reporter may not understand the process of sequencing. Coach the reporter to first set a goal for a story or project and then determine the sequence of steps to carry it out.
Changes in priorities or deadlines for stories in progress or in procedures for working with equipment	This is often caused by poor communication from those responsible for the changes.	Make sure you provide all reporters, producers, or broadcast news personnel with complete information. When you communicate a change, ask for confirmation to be certain everyone understands the new task, the new instructions, and the new deadline.

13 | Coaching to Improve Competence and Performance

After you finish this chapter, you will be able to:
- Decide when to coach
- Evaluate your coaching abilities
- Evaluate each reporter's coaching needs
- Help a reporter set goals to improve performance

Introduction

Coaching is a powerful resource to improve writing, enterprise development, initiative, and creativity as well as enhance performance in today's fiercely competitive environment. Reporters are receptive because you're providing career-enhancing skills in a nonthreatening atmosphere. And it's one of the best tools available to you to reduce direct supervision. However, coaching should not be considered one more occasional item to add to a morning meeting agenda. It should be ongoing since, ultimately, the payoff for exceptional coaching is exceptional productivity.

In addition to helping reduce employee turnover, coaching improves the quality and quantity of work by your staff by improving your reporters' problem-solving abilities. Coaching those who report to you to achieve excellence on the job is a fundamental characteristic of your supervisory position and thus a daily task.

It is intricately associated with your role as a leader as well: You are in an optimum position to share your skills with those you work with. You enjoy personal satisfaction in guiding others and unleashing the potential in everyone who reports to you. Coaching enables both you and your staff to anticipate and capitalize on change rather than react to and struggle with it. Editors frequently confuse the coaching function with counseling and disciplining. Others are unable to see the distinction between coaching and teaching. Each is different and has specific goals. (Counseling to change unsatisfactory behavior is discussed in Chapter 10.) Training, teaching, coaching and disciplining are designed to improve performance but each method is different.

Training is formal, step-by-step instruction in a structured environment with lesson plans and specific objectives for achieving a specific proficiency. Training involves instruction over a specified period, usually from one hour to several days, and can include workbooks, handouts, projectors, flip charts, and stand-up presentations. Student understanding is determined by review.[1]

Teaching involves lecture-based tutoring in a classroom setting. Unlike a coach, a teacher may not have first-hand real-world experience with the topic, nor need it. Teaching is designed to add to the learner's knowledge base. Student understanding is determined by test.

Discipline provides information about the consequences of unacceptable behavior. It is generally reactive and attempts to modify or change behavior.

Coaching passes on wisdom by expanding knowledge through hands-on, site-based informal tutoring at times when it is most appropriate. Coaching is interactive instruction and encourages feedback. It is designed to help people develop on the job. Coaching passes on to the learner the skills the coach has personally acquired. Coaching is proactive and can include corrective guidance. Student understanding is determined by on-the-job performance enhancement.

Four Characteristics of an Effective Coach

Although the list of characteristics of an effective coach is extensive, certain traits are necessary to inspire a desire to learn. The following four traits, gleaned from extensive research and observation of successful and effective coaches, emerge as fundamental:

1. Effective coaches are tolerant. Reporters come to the job with different backgrounds, experience, training, senses of humor, ability to understand, work methods, and levels of interest. The effective coach matches the instruction to the individual characteristics of each reporter, producer, or broadcast newsperson.
2. Effective coaches are motivators. Motivation works best when it is selective. Just as pepper is most effective when it is sprinkled sparingly

into soup, motivation is most effective when it is sprinkled lightly into each reporter's workday. The most effective motivation is that which encourages reporters to take personal responsibility for the success of the project. The most effective motivators encourage those who report to them to practice self-motivation by providing the tools, the plan, and the goals the reporter needs to become enthusiastic.

3. Effective coaches are planners. Before beginning a session, the effective coach plans the material, taking each reporter's traits into consideration, and then plans the session in the same way a supervisor would map any other plan to achieve an objective.
4. Effective coaches are evaluators. They set their expectations for each employee based on individual strengths, which the coach helps to develop, and weaknesses, which the coach gently corrects.

Coaching Skills

Whether you're teaching introductory, intermediate, or advanced writing, research, interviewing, or production skills, three steps are involved in coaching a reporter: Explain, demonstrate, and practice.

1. *Explain.* Begin each session with an introduction to the topic. This may include supporting documentation, slides or powerpoint presentation, a video on the subject, and workbook and handout materials on writing, researching, interviewing, producing, or other skills you coach.
2. *Demonstrate.* Use samples or a CD or video segment or other electronic tools for your demonstration. Show the individual how to apply the technique under discussion, a step at a time.
3. *Practice.* Give the learner an opportunity to practice the new skills on exercises you have prepared and provide before-and-after examples of work that needs improvement.

As a coach, you can help underachievers build up their self-esteem. Often this kind of encouragement is all they need to begin developing their full potential. Encouragement works better than criticism. First, select examples where the individual has done well, then point out places where the person can improve by using the skills you're teaching. This helps encourage reporters who might be reluctant to accept criticism and motivates underachievers.

As a coach, you can encourage high achievers to become better. Even high achievers need to be motivated and sometimes corrected as well. The secret to coaching high achievers is to motivate them to maintain their level of excellence. You want the high achiever to serve as a role model for others in the newsroom.

Approach coaching as an opportunity to raise the bar and develop higher performance standards. Your ultimate objective is to encourage rather than discourage, to motivate every person to produce the best they are capable of, and then to improve from there to a new level.

Coaching is a learned skill. If you are unsure about your coaching ability, a self-assessment tool can help you identify areas to improve.[2]

Barriers to Learning

A major barrier between the coach and the learner is fear of the unknown. Learners may dread coaching because they fear they won't understand or will give the wrong answer during the session. This can cause learners to assume a passive role as skills or procedures are explained. They may refuse to ask questions out of fear of appearing unknowledgeable or incompetent, or struggling to understand concepts. So they decide silently to figure it out later rather than ask the coach to explain something they didn't understand.

Another barrier to learning is the difficulty a learner may have trying to absorb too much information at one time. If you load too much information into a single session, the learner may not protest, assuming (erroneously) that others have been taught this way before and have understood. As a result, the learner may make a supreme effort to absorb large chunks of information while barely keeping up with the instruction.

A different kind of barrier to learning can arise when the coach is also the boss: The employee can become defensive. In some cases, if you become impatient with a slow learner, the learner may interpret your behavior as the boss demonstrating superior knowledge.

You'll need to keep one other serious, though subtle, barrier in mind, and it's not a learner's barrier. This is failing to adapt to the pupil's learning style. Each person learns at a different pace. Some people function best in the morning; others are afternoon people. Some people can absorb an entire lesson in one session and apply what they learn immediately. Others may need to attend several sessions so they can learn and practice a step at a time.

As you develop your skills, you will learn how to adapt your coaching style to each person's specific learning style. Keep in mind that coaching is learner-focused rather than instructor-focused. Coaching is another tool you use to achieve results. Therefore, the needs of the learner are paramount.

Assessing the Needs of Learners

You are probably aware of the needs of each person on your staff to improve performance, technology skills, writing or production skills, or other competencies in your newsroom. You may often remind yourself that you must do something about coaching one of these days. The problem with procrastination is that, when you finally decide to spend some time with one or more individuals, you may have forgotten exactly what skill areas the person needs help with. What's worse, over time you may forget which person received what coaching and as a result cover the same ground several times.

You can avoid this by keeping a competency needs list—a roster of each person in your newsroom along with a checklist of the individual's coaching needs. When you're ready to coach this person, or when the individual comes to you for assistance, you will have a program of instruction ready, as well as details on coaching already done and when.

Use the form in Figure 13.1 to track the coaching needs of your staff, the coaching you've accomplished, the date, and the short-term and long-term effects.

An Effective Coaching Session

Because coaching passes on to the learner the skills you have acquired, it offers you an opportunity to do much more than share your technical expertise. At its finest, coaching offers an opportunity to communicate values. You can convey the principles of ethical journalism as well as the company's and your personal values during coaching sessions.

Preparation

Create a positive atmosphere. Begin the session with an icebreaker to put the learner or learners at ease.[3] Empathize with your pupil's needs: They want to learn and to improve. Start the session with a brief summary of your background to establish your authority as a journalist rather than a boss correcting employees.

Coaching means meeting a specific need, generally by changing barely adequate or substandard performance to performance that is more productive. Use the technique of moving from the familiar to the unfamiliar: Find out first what the learners want to know by asking them questions at the outset. Your goal is to establish an interactive atmosphere that gets the learner actively involved.

Coaching

Figure 13.1 Tracking Staff Coaching Needs

Name	Coaching Need	Date	Short-Term Follow-Up (6 Months)	Long-Term Follow-Up (Two Years)

	Beginning (B) or intermediate (I):
	  Computer skills
	  Software skills
	  Production skills
	  Broadcast skills
	  Editing skills			

	New technology or equipment training			
	Ability to write tight copy			
	Ability to write tight radio spots			
	Ability to produce radio spots			
	Ability to write tight video spots			
	Ability to produce video spots			
	Ability to research			
	Ability to search on line			
	Ability to cooperate on team projects			
	Discipline and control			
	Problem-solving skills			
	Planning and organizing skills			
	On-time delivery of assignments			
	Enterprise (creative story development)			
	Interacting with others			
	Achieving superior results			
	Decision-making skills			
	Managing time			
	Interviewing skills			

Demonstrate

Combine lecture with demonstration of the techniques. Tell what you are going to teach, teach it, and then tell what you taught.

Encourage constant participation. Frequently reward correct answers with compliments such as, "Yes, that's very good," or "That's right." If a person gives a wrong answer, don't say, "That's wrong." Instead, say, "That's one way of looking at it. Here's another," and then provide the answer you expected.

Don't confuse the learning process with the reporter's ability to comprehend. If the learner just doesn't get it, even after several explanations, your coaching technique may need adjustment. Try a different approach. And keep trying.

Review the topic or technique from beginning to end. Don't assume the learner is familiar with each part of the process. Help the learner understand the relationship between what is being taught and the broader picture. It is possible that, although the learner is familiar with certain steps, he or she may have been carrying them out improperly. That could be part of the learner's problem if there have been gaffes in past work. Teach the how as well as the why. Let the learner blunder initially—mistakes can be corrected. Mistakes are the building blocks of growth.

Follow-Up

Coaching is never finished. Information must be reinforced. People forget as much as a fourth of what they learn within 24 hours after instruction. A month later, they've forgotten up to 80 percent. In a week or so after a coaching session, check how the learner is progressing.

Ten Principles of Effective Coaching

1. *Make coaching important.* Schedule regular meetings. Don't take phone calls or messages and avoid interruptions during the session. Learners may feel they are less important when their session is interrupted. Take several five- or ten-minute breaks to attend to other business.
2. *Set an objective and stay focused on it.* Effective coaches are results-oriented; they know that those who don't set goals are unable to measure results.
3. *Emphasize ability.* Focus primarily on the strengths of the reporters, producers, or broadcast news personnel you coach. Point out how they can do better with the techniques you are teaching. Reinforce what your people are already doing well. Affirmation is empowerment.

4. *Be flexible.* Allow the flow of the conversation to determine the framework of your coaching session. The meeting will move along at its own pace as the material under discussion develops.
5. *Promote interaction.* Provide for give and take, for listening and answering. In some sessions you'll do much of the talking; in others, much of the listening. Encourage participation with open-ended questions such as what, where, how, and when. For example, "Tell me how you learned to do it this way."
6. *Seek solutions.* Always strive to improve your coaching technique to present information more clearly, and ask for input from your reporters to help you accomplish this.
7. *Focus on the learner.* A good coach knows that each individual is different; an exceptional coach knows what each individual needs.
8. *Share the wealth.* Let others in your newsroom know when a learner has achieved positive results. Improving self-esteem is integral to improving performance.
9. *Build values as well as skills.* Whenever possible, show the relationship between ethical journalism and the skill you are teaching.
10. *Encourage team awareness.* Make it clear that, to be accepted as players on your team, everyone in your newsroom needs to be fully involved. Encourage everyone who reports to you to assume responsibility for coaching colleagues.

Team awareness in your newsroom is more than a group of reporters, producers, photographers, or broadcast news personnel getting along with each other. It is working as a team and is essential, especially on a major story. As supervisor, you both head that team and are a member of it. In the next chapter we examine the importance of team building in your newsroom and how to attain a cohesive team.

Notes

1. Training is discussed in Chapter 17.
2. A list of publishers of assessment tools appears in the appendix.
3. The purpose of an icebreaker is to put the participants at ease and overcome reticence to participate. An effective icebreaker I use to start training sessions is to announce the topic, then break the group into pairs or teams, depending on the size, and assign a spokesperson for each. I ask them to discuss what they would like to accomplish during the session. After two or three minutes of discussion with each other, they review their goals with me as I write them on a flipchart or chalkboard. You achieve three results: You establish clear objectives for the session, uncover needs you may not have been aware of, and initiate interaction.

14 Team Building

After you finish this chapter, you will be able to:
- Establish team goals
- Understand the seven characteristics of effective teams
- Determine how much responsibility for self-direction to grant to your team
- Prepare a team mission statement to accomplish objectives

Introduction

More than at any time in the past, reporters, photographers, producers, and broadcast news personnel are working on investigative and other stories as a team. Technology is changing the way people work so rapidly and thoroughly that reporters are able to coordinate their work with each other and with the newsroom electronically. Moreover, reporters in today's newsroom are better educated, more discerning, more intelligent, and better prepared than at any time in journalism's history. This doesn't mean reporters don't need supervision; it means they need less.

Team coordination is essential to cover a major story, and as editor you are in charge of that team. You direct a large staff, assigned to different aspects of events such as the visit of a world leader, a major political or social event, a mass march in your city, a riot, or other similar events. Coverage requires synchronizing the activities of writers, producers, video camera operators, photographers, rewrite, support personnel, administrative assistants, IT personnel, couriers, drivers, even pilots. Putting together a smoothly functioning team of journalists with different backgrounds, skills, and even diverse motivations requires deft balancing to get the job done right. It's a big job but it's carried out successfully just about every day somewhere.

You don't need to wait for a major event to develop a cohesive team. You can achieve your goals more easily if you bolster team spirit in your newsroom. Team spirit helps reduce newsroom tension; increases respect for others; helps suppress selfishness, sarcasm, and criticism; and moderates office politics. Enhancing team awareness in your newsroom now will make preparing for and covering a major event that much easier.

Your role changes when you lead a team. You are less a boss who gives orders and more a team member who provides guidance, motivation, and inspiration. To be able to operate in that role, you will have to build a team that can

- Adapt easily to change and new technologies
- Help design newsroom strategies to improve productivity
- Enhance the quality of the news report
- Participate in developing team goals
- Meet or exceed goals regularly

None of this is going to happen automatically; groups of reporters don't become more competent because they are now called a team. And although much has been said about the value of teams, they are not an instrument to correct endemic problems. Nor can team cooperation be accomplished overnight. Success doesn't come from telling a group of journalists that they are now a team and then ordering them to begin working as a team. Team members need to know how to solve problems and understand how teams function effectively. Teamwork is something that must be allowed to develop slowly to transform a group of headstrong journalists into an efficient, productive entity. Support from top management must come in the form of a strong commitment to develop and train teams to meet your organization's goals.

The Value of Teams

Why should you invest time and effort in molding your newsroom into a team? Because people are more motivated when they have a say in what they do and how they do it. Individuals respond more positively to an editor who asks for their opinion on how to accomplish a task as opposed to ordering it. Their ownership of the assignment increases dramatically. Teamwork helps shift more responsibility from editors to reporters. Reporters can be more effective when they work together and function as a team than when they act on their own, especially on big stories that require lots of people.

Journalists treasure their independence, so they will initially find the team environment unnatural. It's not easy for them to mold themselves into a smoothly cooperating and unified unit. But the payoff is tremendous and worth the effort.

To succeed as a team, members must

- Pitch in with extra effort for the benefit of the story, the project, the team, and the organization
- Place the goals of the group and the organization ahead of personal goals and agendas
- Possess first-class journalistic skills and employ them consistently
- Understand the group's goals and sincerely believe in them

The successful team also requires a leader who can help the group shape its team goals while synchronizing those goals with the organization's overall objectives, and guide the team in succeeding in achieving the objectives it sets for itself.

Building Newsroom Teams

You are more likely to succeed in building and maintaining a team if you are able to distinguish skill levels, experience, motivation, and willingness to work as a team among the individuals who report to you. You and your team need to change some old ideas and practices and strive to accept and live by new concepts. Most journalists think in terms of individual achievement rather than accountability as a group. To overcome this, you must recognize and reward contributions to the team's success as frequently as you recognize individual achievement. Journalists like to be told they have done a good job, whether as an individual or as part of a team.

Coordination with management and other editors is also necessary to assure team success. Your superior needs to know the goals you have set for your team and how you plan to meet them. Other editors need to be aware of your efforts to work as a team so that they respect the group as a unit.

You will assume several roles as you build your team. First and most important, you remain the boss. It's important the team know that someone is in charge, someone who can support them by making things happen when necessary. Second, you are a team member who helps out as needed. Third, you function as the team's advisor when necessary.

Spend some time now reflecting on what you want your team to accomplish, and how. Write your expectations in broad statements. Once you have your thoughts written down, refine them and convert them into goals. The seven characteristics of effective teams can help you develop specific statements as you work out your list.

Seven Characteristics of Effective Teams

Whether you are new to team leadership or are already supervising a team in your newsroom, you can improve communication and maximize participation, as well as enrich the daily work experience of every member, by adopting the seven characteristics of effective teams.

Just as an employee needs to be fully informed about the company's requirements for the job, so too a team needs to be fully aware of the expectations of the group as a team. Your job, as the team's leader, is to develop those expectations with input from your superiors and then to make sure every reporter on your team understands them.

Teams are more likely to succeed if members work interdependently, accept both personal and group responsibility for achieving goals, and contribute actively and continually to meet the goals with the resources available.

Clear Objectives

Just as a media organization has clear goals, so too an effective team has clear objectives. The team's objectives must be defined; they are as critical in importance to the group as the overall goals are to the organization. Many managers assume that the goals of teams are identical to the goals of the organization, but although company goals should shape a team's objectives, the team itself should have its own statement of objectives.

Establish your team's objectives, with the collaboration of your superiors, as your first step in building a successful team. If you don't know where to start, apply your company's mission statement to your team's specific area of responsibility. Write your team's objectives:

1. _____
2. _____
3. _____
4. _____

Meet with your staff as a team and discuss these goals. Ask for input and modify the goals so that they become objectives that each member of the team can support enthusiastically. Once the goals have been agreed to, make a copy for each team member.

Clear Tasks

Although team members may clearly understand their own work, they may not be aware of how it fits into the overall picture when they are working as a team on a project. Therefore, when you begin a project, take a moment to define its tasks, and write them down. Then meet with the team to make sure the members clearly understand what the team has been assigned to accomplish.

Flexibility

The members of the team must be flexible, willing to jump in to help out when someone is absent, for example, or work extra hours. Such voluntary cooperation is vital to team success. There will be times when one or more members of the team are not working because of vacations, sickness, maternity leave, flex time, medical appointments, or other reasons. Team members should not wait to be told to fill in or take over a task that another team member has not completed. Other members of the team must step in spontaneously and carry the ball to assure that productivity, deadlines, and quality do not suffer. Team members replace each other temporarily when appropriate; they do not substitute.

Participation

Team members should participate actively in such activities as planning, meetings, and even team self-analysis. Normally, one or two members of the team, as in any unit in society, are more outgoing than others and speak their minds with ease, even when they aren't asked to. Others are likely to be cautious about stepping forward to make suggestions. They may fear rejection of their ideas, which they interpret as looking foolish, however erroneous that assumption. They don't understand—and need to be told—that there are no dumb questions.

Consequently, you must make a special effort to encourage less vocal team members to participate actively. Specifically, this may mean calling on them during meetings, for example, and then waiting patiently, and silently, until they speak. Initially they'll have to struggle with their reticence until they become fully aware that everyone on the team has something important to contribute.

Mutual Recognition

Each reporter is on your team because he or she is the best you could find. Each delivers outstanding performance regularly. You should make clear to them frequently that you value them, and you motivate them with frequent congratulatory messages. Peer recognition is equally vital. It's a special kind of motivator. Athletes, especially those who play on a team, know this. Whether they are in practice or on the field or the court, sports team members continually encourage each other. Your team members should also congratulate each other often on a job well done. As their supervisor, you can encourage the group as a team through your own example by recognizing outstanding accomplishments.

Personal Responsibility

Team members should assume personal responsibility for carrying out the tasks assigned to them. They should report their individual progress toward each project goal to the team leader, whether they are on time and on schedule or not. They need to understand the importance of reporting delays, obstacles, adjustments to plans, or other changes in a timely manner so that you as team coordinator can take steps. There should be no surprises.

Creativity

Team members are expected to do a superb job, of course. But they are also expected to tap their creative talents to seek new, unusual, or better ways for the team to succeed.

Team members should continually look for ways to do their assignments better. If each understands the importance of every other member's contribution to the team's efforts, each would look for ways to enhance the success of other members of the team as well. They would make constructive suggestions (rather than critical observations) about the efforts of other team members.

Team Autonomy

How much responsibility for self-direction should you grant to your team? Quite a bit, if the team is ready for it. One of the decisions you will need to make, together with your superiors, is how much responsibility you feel your team is ready for now. A high level of autonomy carries with it a high level of responsibility for results. Your staff are ready for such responsibility if

- They understand the dynamics of and can work together as a team.
- They understand and routinely comply with your organization's mission statement.
- You are prepared to participate as a member of the team as well as its leader.

Measuring Team Effectiveness

An effective method of keeping the team on track is to establish intermediate milestones to determine progress. Prepare an easily accessible team progress report so you can check off accomplishments on the road to each goal. (See Figure 14.1). Data collection on the team's progress toward goals need not be elaborate. A 3 × 5 card on a bulletin board, or an e-mail, listing results based on reports will be enough. Don't forget to include other shifts if they are involved.

Milestones are results you expect and the dates you expect them to happen. Write in those dates on your calendar as reminders to review progress. Check off when the milestone was achieved or partially met; if it was not, write down the reason. This information can help you identify and recognize team commitment. The team progress report can also help the team measure its own performance as well as determine its success at meeting the goals it has established. An example of the use of the Team Progress Report Card appears in Figure 14.2.

Team and personal success should be synonymous. Make sure all members know their own responsibilities as well as their teammates' assignments to assure smooth coordination. As long as everything runs smoothly, your principal role will be to eliminate obstacles, since reporters, producers, or broadcast news personnel will have the authority to make decisions on their own to meet team goals. As the team develops confidence, the skill, self-motivation, and competence of each member will increase. These are the hallmarks of truly successful teams, and they make it possible for the team to stretch to meet or exceed new goals.

Your contributions to help your staff work effectively as a unit are an essential element of your leadership style. You can take justifiable credit for the success of the team you build.

As members of a cohesive team, your staff will deal with customers as well as with each other. Customer service is an area that journalists may not feel applies to them, but it is critical for success. Awareness of customers and a commitment to constantly improve service to them is essential. In the next chapter we look at who the customer is and why it is so important to develop in your people an awareness of the importance of the customer.

Figure 14.1 Team Progress Report

Record of Achievement

Objective #1: _____

Milestones

#1	#2	#3	#4

Team Results: Record of achievement

Review Date	Shift	Date Done	Achieved	Exceeded	Partial	Delayed (Reason)

Objective #2: _____

Milestones

#1	#2	#3	#4

Team Results: Record of achievement

Review Date	Shift	Date Done	Achieved	Exceeded	Partial	Delayed (Reason)

Objective #3: _____

Milestones

#1	#2	#3	#4

Team Results: Record of achievement

Review Date	Shift	Date Done	Achieved	Exceeded	Partial	Delayed (Reason)

Figure 14.2 Example of Use of a Team Progress Report Card

Sample card

Team Progress Report

Project: <u>Roundup of houses built before 1900 in the city for mid-September Sunday magazine</u>

Record of Achievement

Objective #1: <u>Houses in downtown area</u>

Milestones

| #1 June 15 Identify all houses built before 1900 | #2 June 30 Finish contacting all owners to interview | #3 July 15 Finish interviews with at least 50% owners | #4 July 30 Finish interviews with owners of all houses that will be in story |

Team Results: Record of achievement

REVIEW DATE	SHIFT	DATE DONE	ACHIEVED	EXCEEDED	PARTIAL	DELAYED (REASON)
June 15	Dayside only	Not done			One fourth of owners contacted	Some owners don't respond to calls; sent letters
June 30	Dayside only	Not done	Failed to achieve goal; settled for partial goal		Some owners refused to cooperate	Settled for about half of goal of all identified houses
July 15		July 10		Finished half of interviews		
July 30	Dayside only	Not done			Interviews will be finished August 10	Some owners are still unavailable, out of town, or want to fix up the house first.

Team Building

Objective #2: __Houses in other areas of city__

Milestones

#1 June 15 Identify all houses built before 1900	#2 June 30 Finish contacting all owners to interview	#3 July 15 Finish interviews with at least 50% owners	#4 July 30 Finish interviews with owners of all houses that will be in story

Team Results: Record of achievement

Review Date	Shift	Date Done	Achieved	Exceeded	Partial	Delayed (Reason)
June 15	Dayside only	Not done			Only about 10 houses have been identified outside downtown.	Some houses have been destroyed, others are now used for businesses. Two have been moved elsewhere.
June 30	Dayside only	June 30	10 houses have been identified. Three owners will cooperate			Letters or calls to 10. Only three have responded.
July 15		Not done			Only five have been interviewed	Some owners are on vacation.
July 30	Dayside only	July 30			Some houses have not been located. Story will cover those that have been identified.	Addresses of destroyed houses cannot be verified. One is now a warehouse. Another is a bed and breakfast. All owners of converted houses have been interviewed.

(continued)

Objective #3: __Photograph all houses that will be featured in the roundup__

Milestones

#1 June 15 Identify all houses built before 1900	#2 June 30 Finish contacting all owners to interview	#3 July 15 Finish interviews with at least 50% owners	#4 July 30 Finish interviews with owners of all houses that will be in story

Team Results: Record of achievement

Review Date	Shift	Date Done	Achieved	Exceeded	Partial	Delayed (Reason)
June 15	Dayside and second shift	Not done				Photographers have not yet looked at the houses.
June 30	Dayside and second shift	Not done	Failed to achieve goal		Some owners refuse to cooperate	Pictures have been taken of those houses where owners have cooperated.
July 15	Dayside and second shift	Not done			Finished over half of assignment	Pictures have been taken of all houses in the story. Photographers are waiting for some owners to return.
July 30	Dayside and second shift	July 25		All photographs taken and all releases signed and in file.		

15 | Exceeding Customer Satisfaction

After you finish this chapter, you will be able to:
- List your organization's four types of customers
- Understand the importance of customer-first service
- Inspire reporters to exceed customer expectations consistently
- Motivate reporters to maximize their commitment to quality

Introduction

Although customer awareness has not been traditionally within the purview of journalism, it is now and it will become increasingly vital as competition for customers intensifies among traditional media as well as between traditional and electronic media. Newsroom staff may think of customer service as the department in the company where customer service representatives take orders, or handle complaints about advertising or missed deliveries. But the definition of a news organization customer is much more comprehensive than merely someone who pays for an ad or a copy. Customers fit into four categories at any news organization.

The Four Types of Customers

The *current* customer is the one who takes out an advertisement, buys your publication, selects your news show or on-line service, or purchases any product your organization offers for sale, such as books or services.

The *potential* customer is someone who might purchase your organization's products or services, including those who made purchases in the past but have not recently done so.

The *universal* customer is everyone who doesn't fit into the first two categories. This is anyone who might come in contact with the news division of your organization anywhere, anytime, for any reason. Readers, viewers, and listeners, for example, are customers of your organization's news content. So are people your reporters interview.

Other people your reporters might come in contact with are sales people at a supermarket, gas station, or a community event. Supermarket shopping might sound like a strange venue to assure customer satisfaction, but in fact, the reporter represents the newspaper, magazine, or station wherever that reporter goes. If the reporter is curt at the checkout counter, for instance, the store employee does not remember the individual responsible for the brusque treatment. After that discourteous reporter leaves, the supermarket employee turns to a colleague and complains, "Did you see how I was treated by Channel Seven?"

Finally, the *internal* customer is everyone in your organization. That is, anyone in your organization who requests a service from one of your reporters is an internal customer of that reporter. Internal customers are also those in your organization who provide a service for your reporters. Those people include the switchboard operator, engineers responsible for the newscast on radio or television, photographers, and news anchors. It includes personnel in sales, accounting, typesetting, production, printing, and delivery.

Customer Awareness

Because the customer is anyone outside your organization or in it, including reporters, everyone must be constantly prepared to provide quality service to everyone else. Customer service is, in reality, customer *awareness*. Whether or not they feel they are in direct contact with customers, all reporters must be constantly aware of them, no matter what role that customer plays.

Your organization delivers a two-part product—news and advertising (or sponsorship if nonprofit)—for its customers through the medium that conveys it, whether it is a newspaper, magazine, or broadcast signal. Ultimately, your department is responsible for its contribution to the customer's satisfaction with the news and information half of the product that your organization sells. The success of that product depends on customer acceptance, and *that* depends on two fundamentals: the quality of the product and the commitment to the customer.

As editor, you should explain to those who report to you who your customers are. Develop in your people an awareness of the importance of *all* the customers. Your goal is to get them committed to delivering a quality news product that brings customers back.

Quality

Have you ever attempted to define quality? Take a moment now to write down your definition of quality, then compare it with the definition that follows.

My definition of quality: _____

_____

_____

One dictionary defines quality as the *character of excellence.*[1] Notice this definition does not say quality is *a* characteristic of excellence. The distinguishing—and only—attribute of quality, according to this definition, is excellence. That excellence derives from inherent character.

Quality and character in the news report, like the quality and character of the reporters who produce it, develop from within. Quality in today's newspapers, magazines, and broadcasts ranges from mediocre to superb, depending on who's defining and who's delivering it. Quality is a nebulous entity, perceived and defined by the customer who equates integrity with quality, evaluating your news report and comparing it with what you promised to deliver. Ultimately, quality is merely a buzzword if it is not consistently excellent. Excellence, in fact, is a synonym for quality. And there is only one method to assure excellent quality: to commit to it. Every reporter must be committed to producing excellence consistently.

Understanding Commitment to Quality

No one ever said motivating commitment is an easy task. Before you can motivate others, both you and they need to understand what commitment means.

Can you define commitment? Take a moment to write in your definition of commitment, then compare it with the suggested definition that follows:

My definition of commitment: _____

_____

_____

Returning to the dictionary once more, we find one definition of commitment is "to give over to another for a purpose such as care or safekeeping."[2] This suggests that customers place their confidence in you, trust you, and rely on your integrity.

Many editors would contend that quality is defined by the organization. That is, you (as the producer of the product) define the quality of the product for the customer.

Do you agree? If you do, your answer is characteristic of management in many media organizations. But it's a mistake to think that, as creators of the news report, you are the only arbiters of what constitutes quality in a story. Ultimately, it is the *customer* (reader, viewer, or listener) who decides whether your news product meets the customer's standards of quality. One way customers confirm their evaluation of the work you produce is when they regularly prefer your publication or watch or listen to your broadcast. In other words, customers keep coming back. This is often referred to as the *loyalty effect*.

Commitment to quality is not your commitment to the customer, it's the customer's commitment to you. The customer defines the quality of your product or service. You and your reporters define the quality of the work you do that produces that product. The customer commits to an expectation of integrity in your work and that of your reporters. When a customer buys what you offer (reads, listens, or views), the customer is placing trust and confidence in you to produce the highest quality news product possible. That news product should consistently exceed the highest standards of journalism. It is produced by a passion for excellence.

Defining a Passion for Excellence

The word for passion in Japanese is *netsui*. Commitment to quality is not a statement; it's an attitude, a passion, a *netsui* for excellence in everything the reporter does, all day, every day. One way to stress a commitment to quality work in your reporters is to ask them: "How good is the best you can do? Is this story your best? If it isn't, make it so."

Here's an anecdote that may help impress the issue of quality on your reporters. Suppose you've boarded a large jet for a long cross-continent flight. Mistakenly toggling a switch, the pilot inadvertently broadcasts to the passengers his conversation with the copilot. "I sure had a bad night," the pilot tells the copilot, as the passengers listen. "I'm exhausted. I don't feel like doing a good job today." Imagine how you would feel if you heard such a comment coming from the captain of your jet as it takes off. Well, assume the customer feels the same way about your news product. "I trust you to do the best job you can this one time." That's the customer's expectation, whether it's an airline flight, an article in print, an electronic article, or a broadcast.

Customers expect your journalists to fulfill what amounts to an implied promise of integrity and excellence. That's the goal; that's commitment to excellence.

Improving Reporters' Attitudes Toward Readers

One way to train your reporters to improve their attitude toward customers is to explain the CUSTOMER C.A.R.E.© formula: commit, accept, respond, empathize.

COMMIT

Focus all day long on the primary objective of the organization: to serve and satisfy customers. Companies that don't have customers don't have payrolls, either.

ACCEPT

Treat people as they come to you, not as you would like them to be or think they ought to be. Difficult or demanding customers should be respected for their discernment in selecting a company that provides such high quality. Avoid pigeonholing customers as "difficult" or "easy." Even easy-to-please customers should never be taken for granted.

RESPOND

Act quickly to correct any problems customers might have. Each reader or viewer feels he or she is the most important customer you have. Immediate and satisfactory response is the only way to convey your commitment to your customer. Commitment to understanding and resolving a particular customer's issue should be the only thing on your mind. No one expects the impossible, of course, but do whatever you can to meet your customer's needs as quickly as possible. Putting off dealing with customer complaints until other work is finished may cause you to end up with few customers to finish work for.

EMPATHIZE

Identify with your customers by trying to put yourself in your customer's place when there are complaints to your department. Imagine how you would feel, as a customer, if the incident being described had happened to you. Then do what you expect would be done for you, every time.

Exceeding Customer Expectations

To reassure customers, your reporters and you must be prepared to do whatever it takes to meet or exceed every expectation, solve every problem. That means every person in your newsroom should follow up when necessary, even if it's extra research, exhaustive review, or other work. Make sure your people understand they must maintain a concerned, committed attitude toward each customer that your company has. That means everyone who comes in contact with you, your people, your organization, or your news product.

Continuous commitment to excellence is what ultimately produces an attitude of customer-first awareness, whether the reporter is writing a story, interviewing a source, or meeting the needs of a colleague.

The reporter *is* the organization wherever he or she goes. Make certain each reporter understands and practices that.

You can help reporters achieve continuous excellence by making sure everyone in your organization receives continuous training and development. In the next chapter we look at one of the most pleasant activities you will enjoy as an editor: passing on your experience and know-how to promising reporters, producers, photographers, or broadcast news personnel.

Notes

1. The Random House Dictionary of the English Language, The Unabridged Edition, New York, 1967, definition 3: "character with respect to excellence, fineness, etc. . . ."

2. American Heritage Dictionary of the English Language, 3rd Edition, Houghton Mifflin Company, 1992, Electronic Version 1994, Infosoft International, Inc.

16 Training Reporters

After you finish this chapter, you will be able to:
- Prepare effective lesson plans for trainees
- Practice techniques to maintain interest during a training session
- Use a three-step approach to assure clear instruction
- Present a productive training session

Introduction

In the first section of this book, we reviewed techniques for finding and interviewing the right people and then matching them with the right job. You'll also want to upgrade a reporter's present skills to meet the requirements of the job, the beat, or your organization's expectations and reputation for excellence. Training helps accomplish this. Given enough time, reporters may learn on their own of course, but training is more efficient. Training assures you the reporters have the skills you require, plus it gives them the opportunity to learn additional skills they need. Training helps good reporters become even better researchers, interviewers, writers, or producers who work with increased ease, sophistication, care, and precision.

Moreover, training is no longer optional; training is a necessity. Reporters who receive advanced training are highly motivated, more productive, more likely to be satisfied employees, and more likely to continue working in your organization. Well-trained reporters, producers, photographers, and broadcast news personnel advance more quickly in their careers. Trained people produce a superior news report, your newsroom sparkles, and so do you.

Yet some editors question the need for training. They expect reporters, producers, photographers, and broadcast news personnel to know how to do the job they were hired for. Other editors train their staff only because management decrees it or out of desperate dissatisfaction with seriously unacceptable work.

Done well, training can benefit your reporters tremendously by helping them increase their effectiveness. Done poorly, it can trigger a false sense of security in the trainer and the student alike, who presume performance should improve simply because information was exchanged.

Training Benefits Everyone

You will need to spend some time studying effective training techniques and then practice them repeatedly to become proficient. You don't know how to train well just because you know how to do something well. Editors are skilled practitioners, but expertise does not necessarily make them effective trainers. There's a world of difference between knowing how to do a task and effectively teaching someone else how to do it. Telling isn't training.

You don't need to go back to school to learn how to be a good trainer (although attending a seminar or reading a book on the subject wouldn't hurt).[1] But your training sessions will be much more interesting and trainees will benefit more from them if you learn a few presentation techniques.

In most cases, the reporter, producer, photographer, or broadcast newsperson is already familiar with the fundamentals of the job. Training will refine or improve writing, editing, production, or technical skills, as well as introduce new procedures.

It's unlikely that you will have time to train those who report to you on every element they need help with. Therefore, you ought to set your own parameters for training now. Decide what areas you will concentrate on to assure your staff produces an accurate, well-written, well-produced news report.

Designing and Delivering a Training Session

As an editor, you should not attempt all training yourself. Training on the use of sophisticated software programs or electronic equipment, for example, is better left to experts in their fields. Your newsroom training will fit into one of three broad categories:

- *Distinguish* (example: how to recognize good writing and bad writing)
- *Solve* (example: how to make difficult or complicated information easy to understand)
- *Develop* (example: how to research efficiently or find the right information quickly).

Your first task is to distinguish between what reporters do well and where they need to improve. One way to determine areas you want to concentrate on is to ask yourself, "After the training is finished, what should the reporters, producers, photographers, or broadcast news personnel be able to do?" Select from the following list of areas in news writing where you may want to help writers improve, and add your own:

- Eliminate cliches
- Improve color in writing
- Improve leads
- Improve style
- Avoid shifts in tone in writing
- Use scrupulously accurate quotes
- Understand libel law

The training session should be held in a room where you can combine lecture and visual presentation such as an overhead projector with sample sentences or paragraphs projected from a transparency, for example. (You can show how to improve copy with a marker right on the transparency, or you can project a file from a PC and work directly in the file.)

Set aside a block of time for your training session when you will not be interrupted. Be sure you have all the materials you will need for the training session. If you plan to use a manual or CD for software training and you have only one copy, work side by side with one trainee at a time using the same manual for reference, or burn more CDs if you have the license or right to.

Begin by identifying the type of learning activity you will use when you prepare your sessions: lecture, question-and-answer, exercises, or a combination. Determine in advance whether you will need more than one practice session, and whether you will need to cover some elements with lecture as well as one-on-one training.

Divide each segment of each training session into two modules:

1. Introduction to the subject you are going to cover
2. Step-by-step instruction

Rather than dictating, "Here's how this is done," plan to pause frequently to explain why this particular way of doing the task is the right way. Explanations help understanding as well as increase retention, especially when there are a number of steps to learn.

Select places in your leader's guide where you can pause during the training to allow the trainee to absorb the information and to ask questions. Ask, "What questions do you have?" which is open-ended rather than "Do you have any questions?" which might get a simple "no" answer.

Build questions into the training session to help you determine the progress your trainee is making as well as to permit interaction. If you get an answer to a question that misses the point, for example, don't tell the trainee the answer was wrong. This discourages. Rather, say something encouraging: "Well, that's one way of doing it. Here's another way you'll find more effective." Summarize frequently as well.

Avoid using words such as "mistake," "fail," "error," "wrong." Use words that are positive and enhance the trainee's motivation, such as "excellent" or "that's good" or "that's better."

Use the form in Figure 16.1 as a guide when you prepare a training session.

Figure 16.1 Designing a Training Session

Your objectives for this course:

_____

_____

_____

Analyze the needs of the trainees and list them. This will serve as your guide to develop the course content for each session.

Schedule of training topics:

1. _____
2. _____
3. _____
4. _____

Specific areas where trainees need instruction:

1. _____
2. _____
3. _____
4. _____

Lecture segments. For example: poor writing and how to improve it:

1. _____
2. _____
3. _____
4. _____

(An excellent book to use for training sessions on good news writing is *The Word, The Associated Press Guide to Good News Writing,* Rene J. Cappon, published by The Associated Press, 50 Rockefeller Plaza, New York, N.Y. 10020, 1982.)

Make sure you build in plenty of demonstrations to show how the topic of instruction should be carried out successfully when you develop your course content. Provide plenty of opportunity for feedback. Add a five-minute break at every hour, keeping in mind that five-minute breaks usually extend to ten.

Preparing for a Training Session

1. Prepare a workbook and make a copy for each trainee. Organize each lesson by pages. Each page should move the material forward a step at a time. Lecture time for a page can last from one to five minutes or longer, depending on the content. Provide space in the handouts for writing notes.
2. Time each page of material. You can do this by rehearsing out loud. Write down how long each segment takes you to deliver, adding a couple of minutes for the trainee to ask questions. Then rehearse again. It should take you less time on the second trial performance. Write down the new, lower time at the top of each page.
3. Write a summary at the bottom of each page or segment. Use this summary to review material you just covered and to segue to the next page or segment.
4. Provide plenty of examples.
5. Combine exercises with lectures.
6. Be alert for waning interest. Change your presentation style from lecture to exercise, role-playing, or group exercise to maintain attention.
7. Practice patience and understanding during the workshop. Not everyone is going to get it the first time.
8. Never underestimate your trainees' intelligence. But never overestimate their knowledge.
9. Aspire to be a superb trainer by following the three rules of public speaking: practice, practice, and practice.
10. Follow up after the training session. Don't expect the reporter to come to you with doubts or questions just because you closed the session with, "If you have any questions, I'm always available."

Training New Reporters

Unless you have a formal training program in your company, it will be your responsibility to train people you hire for their first journalism job. Use your company's job description as an outline or guide for your introductory speech, adding any special information the reporter needs to know for the position. This introduction should include a discussion of ethical journalism and the company code of conduct, including the penalties for infractions. Make all this clear in your initial conversation with the new reporter and you will avoid problems later.

Because it's unlikely that inexperienced reporters, producers, photographers, or broadcast news personnel will produce acceptable work immediately, expect to devote time to intensive on-the-job training during a new hire's first weeks. Even if they have a journalism, communications, or other degree, new reporters may lack real-world journalism experience. Since many of their questions will be basic, practice patience when you answer. Try to avoid ego-deflating comments such as, "I told you that yesterday" since information will be piling on so fast they will have a hard time remembering everything. Some of their questions will be so fundamental that you will have to interrupt your work and provide elementary instruction before the new reporter can continue working.

Recent graduates from even the most prestigious journalism schools will come to you with little experience working in a media organization, although they may have worked as interns elsewhere or done freelance work. Most teenagers have had some part-time or full-time job experience, but those jobs generally don't prepare them for the pressure cooker environment of a modern newsroom. Some may have had little work experience, so be empathetic as well as firm when you explain that a deadline does not mean two minutes later.

Give new reporters, producers, photographers, or broadcast news personnel opportunities for frequent feedback. When you assign the new person tasks or duties, include specific deadlines. Log the newcomer's progress as the assignments are completed. Catch and correct mistakes immediately: don't wait for the performance appraisal interview, six months or a year later. Some editors like to think that new reporters will learn by doing, but inexperienced people need close guidance.

The best way to monitor a new person without appearing to be hovering is to assign an experienced newsroom person as a mentor. Mentors can quickly respond to questions, and they can coach and monitor at a pace suited to the newcomer. The mentor can keep an eye on how the new reporter handles the job both inside and outside the newsroom, and can even accompany the reporter on a few interviews or research assignments.

Another method to check on progress is to prepare a quiz for the new person after a few weeks on the job. The quiz can be verbal, written, or a test assignment, such as, "Show me how you would write a second-day lead for this story when you have no new information."

In a tight labor market, you may have to hire reporters, producers, photographers, or broadcast news personnel who may be switching careers, people who have not studied journalism in college, or others who may have worked for a media company in the past but in a different capacity. Try to understand each person's background and needs.

Helping reporters, producers, photographers, or broadcast news personnel to do their jobs better or faster is one of the most rewarding aspects of the editor's, news director's, and producer's job when it's done for the right reason: contributing to the reporter's success. Ultimately, your goal as editor, news director, or producer is to motivate maximum performance from each person in your newsroom. Sharing your wisdom and knowledge with those who report to you could well become one of the most satisfying rewards of your career as an editor.

Note

1. A classic book on training techniques is *Presentations Plus,* by David Peoples, John Wiley & Sons, New York, 1988.

Appendix

I. Personnel Policy Manual—Suggested Contents

Employment

Application for Employment
Classification and Compensation
Employment Physical
Equal Opportunity Employment
Total Remuneration and Overtime

Standards and Philosophy

Acceptance of Gifts or Gratuities
Consequences of Harassment of Co-Workers
Conflicts of Interest
Dress Code
Drug-Free Workplace
Food and Beverages in the Workplace and Neatness
Maintaining Confidentiality of Company Information
Nepotism
Outside Employment
Safety
Smoke-Free Environment
Selling Non-Company Goods or Services to Co-Workers or Others

Employee Information and Relations

Dependability and Attendance
Disabling conditions
Discharge for Cause
Discipline
Employee Performance, Evaluation, and Promotion
Employee Status Changes
Orientation and Probationary Period

Procedure for Lodging Complaints or Reporting Problems and Procedure for Resolution
Punctuality

Employee Benefits

Authorized Holidays
Compassionate Leave
Employee Education and Tuition Reimbursement
Jury Duty
Leave of Absence
Military Reservist Status
Paid Time Off
Rest and Meal Periods
Other Benefits

Records and Payroll

Pay Dates and Adjustments for Errors
Personnel Records
Requests for Written References

II. Employee Concern Laws (Laws that Protect Whistleblowers)

Note: The following laws prevent an employer from retaliating against a whistleblower. An employee has 30 days from the date of the suspected retaliation to file a complaint with the Department of Labor.

29 USC 660, Occupational Safety and Health, and related 29 CFR 1977, Occupational Safety and Health Act of 1970
An employer must provide a safe working environment. An employee can ask questions about how the employer is complying with the law.

29 CFR 24, Procedures for Handling Discrimination Complaints Under Federal Employee Protection Statutes

31 USC 3730, False Claims Act
This law was enacted during the Civil War. It deals with companies filing false claims to the federal government. A whistleblower can receive 15 to 39 percent of the amount the federal government recovers as a result of false claims.

42 USC 1983, Civil Action for Deprivation of Rights
This act covers rights guaranteed under the Constitution, such as freedom of speech.

Appendix   195

III. Books, CDs, and Videos

How to Legally Document Employee Discipline, Mike Deblieux. 30-minute video. Includes self-study book, *Documenting Discipline.* Business Advantage, Inc., 4601 121st Street, Urbandale, IA 50323. (800) 305-9004.

Employer's Toolbox. Includes recruitment tools, Attendance Controller, Confidential Employee Record, and other forms. Paper Attendance Controller in binder also available. gneil Companies, 720 International Parkway, Sunrise, FL 33325. (800) 999-9111 or *www.gneil.com.*

Training Needs Assessment Test. Identifies the training needs of managers, supervisors and supervisory candidates. This is a 75-item objective test that pinpoints training needs in 15 key management skill dimensions, including: coaching and counseling, motivation, decision making, planning and organizing, discipline and control, training, leadership, time management, human relations, and communication. Talico Inc., 2320 S. Third Street, Jacksonville Beach FL 32250. (904) 642-0300, Fax (904) 642-7004, *www.talico.com*

IV. Forms and Documents

Your human resources department will keep many, perhaps all, of the following forms on file, generally for one year. Find out which forms you will be expected to keep on file in your office. Make sure all forms have been filled in as required by law. Keep up to date on new legislation as well as changes in federal and state laws to be sure you and your organization are meeting all requirements.

Check current applicable federal and state laws for each document to determine how long you must keep each document on file from the date you received it.

Accident and safety records
Accommodation requests under the Americans with Disabilities Act ADA
Advertisements for jobs
Aptitude tests
Attendance records
Background checks
Descriptions of jobs
Equal Employment Opportunity EEO-I reports
Exit interviews
Grievance reports

Insurance claims
Medical records
OSHA 200 records
Payroll records
Performance appraisals
Personality tests
Physical exams
Posters required by law to be displayed
Pre-employment tests
Psychological exams
Records of benefits (health insurance, COBRA, and other benefits)
References
Release forms and waivers
Reports on disciplinary action
Resumes
Skills tests
Tests for drugs and alcohol
Unemployment insurance claims
Worker's Compensation claims

Index

A
Affirmative action laws, 36
Ambition, 114
Appreciation, need for, 57
Assignment session, 27–28
Assignments, 21, 23
   and editors, 25–27
   handling resistance to, 31–33
   pairing, 31
Authority levels, 8–9

B
Behavior. *See also* Emotional outbursts
   encouraging changes in, 139
   leading to disciplinary action, 131
   test, 150
   time management difficulties traced to, 150
   unsatisfactory, 121
      example of, 124
      steps to change, 125
Benefits, company, 50–51
Broadcast Employment Services, 37

C
Candidate Interview Worksheet, using, 40, 41
Candidates, job
   assigning sample stories to, 45, 46
   challenges by, 36
   describing company dress codes to, 42
   follow-up for promising, 47
   identifying reliable sources for, 45
   Internet search for, 42
   methods of recruiting, 37
   objective scoring of, 41
   sample profiles for, 37–39
   selecting right, 35, 47
   testing, 45
Change, 19–20
   anxiety and, 61–62
   counseling, for bad habits, 125
   planning for, 126
   creating atmosphere amenable to, 59
   discussing need to, 127
   elements for successful, 70–73
   establishing milestones during, 72, 128
   of habits, steps to implement, 128
   I To U method of communicating, 67–68
   and improved technology, 63–64
   managing, 73
   in newsroom, 61, 62
   physical, 63
   resistance to, 60, 127
      causes for, 64–65
      managing intense, 69–70
      remedies for, 65–67
   types of, 62–64
Cheerleading, 59
Coaches
   barriers and, 162
   effective, 160–161. *See also* Coaching
Coaching. *See also* Coaches
   benefits of, 159–160
   defined, 160
   effective, 163, 165
   ten principles of, 165–166
   needs, tracking staff, 164
   skills, 161–162
Commitment
   enthusiastic, 139
   long-term employee, 43
   to quality, 181–183, 182
   defining, 181–182
Communication
   basic theory of, 4
   during change process, 70, 72–73
   defined, 3–4
   eliminating problems in, 11–12
   management style and, 20
   new forms of urgent, 146
   of plans and goals, 14
   setting goal for, 8
   skills, improving, 5, 7–9
   styles, 29–30
      understanding, 28–30
   and teams, 170
Company policies, 108
   avoiding and clarifying misinterpretations of, 48, 49–50, 51
   changes in, 62–63
   ensuring understanding of, 49–50
   need for adhering to, 122
   need for clear explanation of, 48
   and reprimands, 123
   responsibility to understand, 52
Complaints, 103
   common mistakes made when investigating, 107

Complaints *(continued)*
  documenting
    investigation of, 107–109
    of similar incidents, 108
  guidelines for handling,
    110–111
  ignoring motivation for, 106
Compliments, 58, 60, 72, 140
  use of, with coaching, 165
Conflict resolution training,
  110
Controls, management, 14
Counseling, 121, 122,
  123–124
  interview, 128
  unsatisfactory performance
    after, 129
Customer, 182
  awareness, 180–181
  current, 179
  expectations, exceeding, 184
  importance of reporters' atti-
    tude toward, 183–184
  internal, 180
  potential, 179
  universal, 180
CUSTOMER C.A.R.E.
  formula, 183

D
Deadlines, 19, 23
Decision making, 98
  checklist for, 97
  defending, 95, 96
  gathering facts before, 92
  process of, 95–96
  use of documentation for,
    92, 96
Direction, management, 14
Disagreement, 11–12
Disappointments, preventing,
  43
Discipline, 121, 122, 130
  aids for, 195
  defined, 160
  formal, 123
  and need for consistency, 124

as responsibility of editor,
  132
Distractions, 8, 11
Documentation
  of complaints, 107–109
  of expectations, 135
  use of, for decision making,
    92, 96
Dress code, 42

E
Editor & Publisher, 37
Editors, 13. *See also*
  Supervisors
  and assignments, 25–27
  avoiding crises, 104
  and communication with
    reporters, 16
  and customer awareness,
    180–181
  effective, and discipline, 132
  and handling of emotional
    outbursts, 113,
    116–117
  and handling of reporters'
    concerns, 104–107
  handling of resistant re-
    porters, by, 31–33
  need for staff encourage-
    ment, by, 58
  new, 103, 104
  and problem solving, 91
  responsibilities of, 25
  role of, with new hires,
    48–52
  successful, presentations
    and, 75
  as team members, 168, 169
  typical daily activities of,
    146–147
Emotional outbursts, 113
  causes of, 114–115
    frustration and, 116
    trying to identify,
      117–118
  dealing with, 116
  statements for, 117

finding solutions for, 119
focusing on underlying
  problem of, 118–119
Employee concern program,
  111
Employee handbook, 52, 122
  suggested contents for,
    193–194
Encouragement, 58, 161
  regular, 60
Environment, 11
  distractions in, 8
  ensuring safe and respectful,
    104
Envy, dealing with, 114
Equal Employment Opportu-
  nity guidelines
  complying with, 35, 36
  exceptions in, 36
  problem areas in, 36
Exit interviews, 43
Expectations, 51
  describing, 32
  discussing, at performance
    review, 139
  documenting, 135
  job candidates and, 42–43
  lowering, 70
  meeting, 136
  reiterating workplace, 123
  reviewing, 140
  team, 169
  understanding, 27–28

F
Failure, learning from, 60
Feedback
  for new hires, 190
  positive, 60, 110
  providing continuous, 7
  in training session, 189
  unsolicited, 58
Files, 153
Filtering, 18–19, 125
Firing. *See* Termination
Forms, list of needed,
  195–196

G

Goals, 13
  acceptance of, 20
  allocation of tasks for, 14
  clear, 18
  communication, 8
  company, describing, 43
  effective, need for, 18
  flexible, 19–20
  general, 15
  organizational, teams and, 168
  realistic, 19
  setting, 140
    reporter's form for, 142–144
    teaching skills for, 15–16
    team, 169, 170
  specific, 15
  specifying, for investigations, 107
  training, 187

H

Hamilton, Dennis, 108
Hearing, 5. *See also* Listening

I

Internal chatter, 9, 11
Interviews. *See also* Performance appraisal, conducting interviews for
  investigative, 107
  planning, 39–41, 47
  procedure, need for impartial, 35
  virtual, 41–42

J

James, William, 124
Jealousy, 118
  triggering, 114–115
Job dissatisfaction, 58
Journalists
  complaining nature of, 103
  and managing change, 57
  mobility of, 42
  reputation of, 29
  rule stretching, by, 123
  as team members, 168–169

L

Layoffs, 63, 119
Leadership
  during changes, 60–61, 73
  and coaching, 159
  criticism of, 116
  effective, 14
  enhancing, through presentations, 75
  by example, 59, 121
  inspirational, 58
Learners
  assessing needs of, 163–165
  barriers and, 162
Listening, 5
  with compassion, 128–129
  exceptional, 9
  filters, 6–7
  inefficient, 9
  at performance reviews, 139
  skills, 10
  tips for better, 11
Litigation, avoiding, 105, 129
Longevity, determining potential, 42
Loyalty, building, 58
Loyalty effect, 182

M

Mackenzie, R. Alec, 145
Management
  functions, 13–14
  senior, 13
    change imposed by, 68–69
  stress, 64
    during change, 70
  style, criticism of, 103
Management, time. *See* Time management

Meaning, of words, 11
  agreement on, 5
Mentors, 190
Mix, balanced, 25
Morale, 99
  improving, 58
Motivation, 160–161, 168
  of commitment, 181–182
  effective, 60
  increasing, 99, 161–162
  opportunities, through presentations, 75
  of performance improvement, 138
  styles, 58–60
  of trainees, 188

N

Netsui, 182
New hires
  feedback for, 190
  orientation session for, 48, 49, 50, 51
  stress of, 48–49
Note taking. *See also* Documentation
  at investigative interviews, 107
  for unsatisfactory behavior, 123

O

Objectives, 13. *See also* Goals
  altering, 19
  establishing clear, 15, 43, 44
  struggle to achieve, 60
  team, 170
Organization, management, 14

P

Performance appraisal, 135, 137–138
  conducting interview for, 138–139
  editor's form for, 140–142

200   Index

Performance apprasial *(continued)*
  reporter's self-evaluation form for, 137
  sessions, 127
Personnel needs, anticipating future, 45, 47
Planning
  for coaching, 161
  formula, 14–15
  importance of daily, 146. *See also* Time management
  management, 13
  a story, 16–17
  for unforeseen events, 17–18
Points of view, differing, 11–12
Practicing, 123
Presentations
  audience at
    considering, 78–79
    maintaining interest of, 83
  determining and emphasizing key points of, 80
  determining objective for, 77
  organization of, 78
  outlines for, 78
  rehearsing, 80
  sample, 84, 85
    worksheet for, 86–87
  successful
    five elements of, 83–84
    keys of, 75
  timing, 80
  topics for, 84
  training, 186. *See also* Training session
  varying, 80
Priorities, setting work, 154
Problem analysis, 99
  principles of, 92
  reporters, and process of, 98

Problem solving. *See also* Problems
  and coaching, 159
  involving reporters in, 98–99
  need for agreement on issue, in, 106–107
  need for prompt decision, in, 105
  procedure for, 92–98
  questioning technique for, 106
  and reporters with personal problems, 128–129
  worksheet for, 99, 100–102
Problems. *See also* Behavior; Problem solving
  behavioral, 119. *See also* Emotional outbursts
  communicating decisions regarding, 96–98. *See also Decision making*
  considering alternatives to, 95
  correctly identifying, 92–93
  emotional, 113–114. *See also* Emotional outbursts
  finding cause of, 94–95
  follow-up to, 98
  personal, in workplace, 128–129
  with reporters, confidential discussion of, 104
  researching, 93–94
  solution to
    choosing, 95–96
    implementing, 96
    no-action, 97–98
Productivity
  coaching and, 159
  damage to, 63
  enhancing, 156
  increasing, 58
Promotions, 63
  ambition and, 114
Prompting, 123
Public speaking, 75. *See also* Presentations
Punishment, 124, 130

Q

Quality, 181
Questions
  anticipating, 8
  at presentations, 79
  asking, to narrow complaint, 111
  types of, for problem solving, 106
  use of, in training session, 187

R

Recognition, 58
  ambition and, 114
  mutual, on teams, 171–172
  need for, 57
Reporters
  angry, typical causes for, 105
  asking for suggestions from, for behavioral problems, 119
  bad habits among, 124
  as cause of problem, 92
  challenges for new, 48–49
  change and, 64–65, 127
  clinging to customs, of, 60
  coaching, 161–162
  communication styles of, 28–30, 33
  concerns of, 106
    categories of, 104
    documenting, 107–109
    ten guidelines for handling, 110–111
  dealing with ambitions of, 114
  dealing with emotional outbursts of, 116–117. *See also* Emotional outbursts
  encouraging positive behavior of, 122–123
  follow-up system for, 21–24
  giving clear message to, 27–28

goal-setting skills and, 16
impact of change on, 61
improving attitude of, toward customers, 183
inclusion of, in change process, 65–67, 72, 127
information for, at assignment session, 27
involving, in problem solving, 98–99
matching, with right stories, 26–27
measuring progress of, 21
motivating, 58–60
need for acceptance of goal, by, 18, 19, 20
and performance reviews, 136–139
preventing filtering, by, 18–19
resistant, 31–33
short- and long-term goals for, 140
forms for, 142–144
team-style, 30
and technology, 167
time management and, 155–156
training new, 189–191
unsatisfactory behavior of, 121
Resistance
to change, 60, 64–65, 127
intense, 69–70
minimizing, 59
by reporters, 31–33
Respect, 104
divisive behavior and, 115
Restructuring, 63
Risk, 60
ROAD method, 16–17
RTNDA *Job Bulletin*, 37

S

Selective memory, 9
Self-esteem, low, 58
building up, 161
dealing with, 115

Self-starters, 29, 60
Spontaneous inspiration, 59
Standards, performance, 14. *See also* Performance appraisal
developing higher, 162
Stories. *See also* Assignments
assigning, 26
energizing, 57
lead, 26
Stress, 64
during change, 70
of new hires, 48–49
Supervision, 121
effective, 60
importance of consistency in, 120
tools for reducing direct, 159
Supervisor
being a sympathetic, 129
dealing with emotional outbursts, as, 116. *See also* Emotional outbursts
defined, 13
managing time effectively, as, 140
problem solving by, 98–99. *See also* Problem solving

T

Tape recording, of investigative interviews, 107
Tardiness, 124, 125, 127, 130
Tasks
distinguishing between urgent and important, 151–154
prioritizing, 154–155
team, 170–171
Teaching, defined, 160
Team
autonomy, 172
building newsroom, 169
change and, 67–68
characteristics for cohesive, 168

characteristics of effective, 170–172
cooperative, 60
coordination, need for, 167
creativity, 172
effectiveness, measuring, 173
flexibility, 171
members, personal responsibilities of, 172
participation of members in, 171
progress report, 174–175
card, example of, 176–178
spirit, 168
-style reporters, 30
Teamwork. *See* Team
Telephone, use of, 154
Termination, 130, 132
Time
devoting, for on-the-job training, 190
limits, for keeping materials, 153
log, 147–148, 149
sample code for, 148
needs, for training session, 187
usage analysis, 146–148, 151
wasters, 147, 151
examples of, 157–158
solutions for, 157–158
Time management. *See also* Time
causes of poor, 150
efficient newsroom, 155–156
problems, self-generated, 151
successful, 151
technology for, 146
Tolerance, 160
Tone of voice, 11
Training
defined, 160
goals for, 187

Training *(continued)*
  necessity of, 185–186
  needs assessment, test for, 195
  newsroom, categories of, 186
Training session
  designing, 187–188
  preparing for, 189

U
Union contracts, 123
Unknown deadline, 105

V
Violence, workplace, 110
Visitors, drop-in, 154

W
Warnings, 121
  verbal, 129–130
  written, 130
Whistleblowers, 106, 107
  laws that protect, 194
  treatment of, 111
Workplace
  complaints, 103
  emotional expression in, 115
  causes of, 114–115, 116
  environment, ensuring safe and respectful, 104
  expectations, 123
  habits, unsatisfactory, 121–122
  personal problems in, 128–129
  violence, 110
Workspace, importance of neat, 153

OHIO UNIVERSITY LIBRARY

Please return this book as soon as you have finished with it. In order to avoid a fine it must be returned by the latest date stamped below. All books are subject to recall after two weeks or immediately if needed for reserve.

CF